GUARD SLIPPING A COACH

PICKING UP MAILS AT SPEED

TRACK SIGNALS

PICKING UP WATER AT SPEED

LOCOMOTIVE HEAD CODES

POINT CONSTRUCTION

STEAM BREAKDOWN CRANE

AUTOMATIC TRAIN
CONTROL SYSTEM

THE
RAILWAYMAN'S
POCKET-BOOK

Introduction by R. H. N. Hardy

CONWAY

A Conway Book

Volume © Conway, 2011
First published in Great Britain in 2011 by Conway, an imprint of
Anova Books Company Ltd
10 Southcombe Street
London W14 0RA

Distributed in US and Canada by:
Sterling Publishing Co., Inc
387 Park Avenue South
New York, NY 10016–8810

10 9 8 7 6 5 4 3 2 1

Produced and conceived by Rupert Wheeler

To receive regular email updates on forthcoming Conway titles, email
conway@anovabooks.com with 'Conway Update' in the subject field.

British Library Cataloguing in Publication Data:
A CIP record of this title is available on request from the British Library

ISBN 9781844861354

Printed and bound by Bookwell, Finland

Publishers Note.
In this facsimile edition, references to material not included in the selected
extract have been removed to avoid confusion, unless they are an integral part
of a sentence. In these instances the note [not included here] has been added.

CONTENTS

INTRODUCTION

After 28 years of retirement following 42 years' service with the London & North Eastern Railway and British Railways, I find myself studying a text that takes me back to the Victorian era and then forward to the LNER Rule Book (1933) that reigned supreme when I started as an apprentice at Doncaster in January 1941. The Editor has chosen well from a large selection of instruction booklets and the task I have set myself is to relate some of the fascinating points raised within this book to my own practical railway life of a slightly later era.

Maurice Vaughan was a GWR engine driver writing from Plymouth in 1893, a year after the Broad Gauge ceased to exist. He writes of the Mutual Improvement Class formed to train the young engineman and such classes were still going strong with the same name up to the end of steam in 1968. But they were always voluntary and although management took a helpful and practical interest, there was no formal training other than profound experience, which made our enginemen such great individualists. Certainly advice and instruction on the job from an Inspector or a Shedmaster helped with the countless lessons to be learned, but formal classroom and workshop experience only arrived with the diesels and electrics.

Vaughan would have been an engineman before the days of the continuous vacuum brake, where every wheel on the train as well as the engine was braked when the driver stopped at a station. But he wrote in 1893 that 'if the vacuum ejector fails, the driver would inform the guard and work the train forward with the hand-brake'. This would mean the fireman and guard working in unison on their hand-brakes, not so comfortable and never to be countenanced today. But it did me good to read of the practice, or it once happened to me with the Westinghouse air brake when the air pump refused duty and at our first call at Clapton, we just managed to stop at the far end of the platform. We knew there was an express due four minutes behind us and that if we hung about, we would delay him. A quick word with the good old guard to ask him to do his stuff on his handbrake, a word to the porter to ring the Wood St depot foreman and off we went hell for leather onto the Chingford branch. We got to Wood St where Jack Barker was waiting with his tools and without further ado he went to the front of the engine to attend to the pump, hanging on with one hand while we climbed the bank up to Chingford. No reports made, no hesitation nor argument – we simply went about our duty to run to time. Jack soon had the pump in order, and of course all the men would have done exactly the same even if I, as District Motive Power Supt., had not been there – I would simply never have heard about it! All through this book you will feel as you read that you are amongst practical men, all members of the 'Great Brotherhood of Railwaymen' to which I am still proud to belong.

I believe that Michael Reynolds was a Locomotive Inspector on the London, Brighton and South Coast Railway when he wrote the early editions of *Locomotive Engine-Driving*, much enhanced by detailed drawings of the famous Stroudley single-wheeler 'Grosvenor' which was built in 1874. It had wooden brake blocks and a powerful steam brake but the LB&SCR had yet to adopt the excellent Westinghouse brake effective throughout the train. For all that, he still used the 'Grosvenor' and the same drawings long after the continuous brake had been introduced. The Westinghouse brake was a joy to operate once you learned to put your faith in that little brake valve which was grasped so comfortably in the hand. One application of 15psi of air was sufficient to make a brisk and perfect stop in the right place once you had the confidence and experience.

Reynolds felt strongly that certificates of proficiency should be introduced to be rigorously earned and to recognise true ability as a means not only of raising the standard of the craft but to enhance the social standing of both driver and fireman. His discourse on the art of engine-driving and of firing is complete

The author on the left with Bryan Gibson, an ex BR colleague, on a LMS Class 2 Ivatt 6441 at Amersham. They were taking part in "Steam on the Met" in 1993.

and he makes the point that firing is as much of an art as driving, but that the driver is in charge and carries the ultimate responsibility for all that takes place in that private world of the footplate.

Some of Reynolds' advice is clearly of its time. For example, he says firmly that no driver must run before time, but I would remind him of the beloved odd minute or two kept 'up the sleeve' by most enginemen. He also says that drivers must not shut the regulator before notching up with the reversing lever. That may have been the case with the Brighton engines, but the best way to get a rupture was to try it on a GN slide valve engine: you could put your foot on that little footrest and haul with legs apart with all your strength but that lever would not budge and no driver that I ever knew would try it on! But elsewhere there are also pertinent points of interest that came down the years to the end of BR steam.

H. A. Ivatt was the Locomotive Engineer of the Great Northern Railway and his little booklet was intended largely for the younger, relatively inexperienced men. It is a clear, friendly and uncluttered work that explains in simple terms how the job should be done. In paragraph 85, Ivatt generously tells the fireman how to get out of trouble when stopped short of steam. In fact, I never heard of this method being put to the test on the rare occasions that we ran short of steam with Ivatt's very free-steaming tank engines on the Bradford expresses. One could reach Morley on time and then get gassed up in three or four minutes with enough steam and water in the boiler to face the climb up to and over the top onto Adwalton Moor. I wouldn't fancy dropping down into Bradford with anything but a brake in prime order!

One rarely reads about picking up water at speed but there is a fair amount to learn from our old friend 'experience'. Driver Bill Thompson and I worked a heavy stopping train from Doncaster to Grantham with one of Mr Ivatt's Atlantics, 4401, a grand engine. Now Bill was a generous man who usually came to work with his pockets stuffed with fruit and as we got near to Muskham troughs, he said: 'Now, Richard, we'll get a drop of water at the "Trawvs" but don't pull the lever down until I shout'. We approached at about 50 mph and I stood at the lever very much at the ready. We ran on to the troughs; on and on and I waited and waited until I felt that Bill must have forgotten, so I pulled the lever. Bill turned his kindly if quizzical face towards me as the lever locked solid and the tank overflowed, the water (and coal) cascading down onto the footplate until there was nowhere to stand and we got a good soaking. As I slaved away at clearing up, a wiser young man, Bill said: 'Never mind, Richard, you'll know better next time – have another apple!' This was one that wasn't in Mr Ivatt's splendid little book.

Next is *Locomotive Management,* often known to railwaymen as *Cleaning to Driving.* The text has been drawn from a 1909 copy, which has a considerable Great Central input: one of the anonymous authors was a Locomotive Inspector and one-time driver, and acknowledgements are made to the Chief Mechanical Engineer and the Running Superintendent of the Great Central Railway as well as to distinguished members of the staff of the Municipal School of Technology in Manchester. I had my first copy new in 1939 but it disappeared over the years; however an up-to-date paperback edition came out a few years ago and is well worth getting, for it is a first rate book.

In Chapter 1, the authors set out to make things clear for the young entrant and advise him to study carefully the shed regulations – and rightly so, although Nos. 1 and 2, for example, could readily be 'bent' as well I know. Stan Hinbest, a Stratford Fitter working under a B17 in the huge double-ended Jubilee Shed has described the feeling when he heard a raft of engines being pushed up his road from the distant back end, wondering how he could get out before the inevitable bump-up. Yet few men were injured, although some, including Stan on another occasion, were very fortunate to escape. No. 2 is pure common sense, which comes automatically to any engineman or shunter berthing an engine for repairs or for going out by and by. But in railway life, there is always the rare exception. When I was in charge at Stewarts Lane in 1954, the little H class tank 1005 had been washed out, cleaned and lit up, ready to go over to Victoria about midnight for 52 duty. Near the outlet of the depot stood a King Arthur, strong and built like a battleship. The driver and Running Foreman were locked in friendly if profane conflict and failed to notice the silent approach of 1005 until there was an almighty bump. Both men vented their fury upon an empty cab for 1005, which had been quietly making steam and decided to move silently down the yard to collide with the big N15. Shed Regulation (2) had been comprehensively neglected but I never did find out who was responsible. Clams to a man!

'Socrates' was Driver Oliver of Nine Elms depot. He was an NUR man and his booklet is comprehensive and very informative, the subject being *The Propulsive Properties of the Steam Locomotive*, published by the NUR in 1923. I thoroughly enjoyed working with the elected representative of the staff whether ASLEF or NUR. As a Shedmaster and later as a District Motive Power Supt., my aim was to raise standards of performance; exactly what the representatives also wanted and often enough for the same reasons.

When we changed over to diesel traction at Stratford everybody had to change their way of life, some 3,000 folk. Jim Groom was the Chairman of the Workshop Committee, a Boilermaker and a born leader, highly regarded at the Boilermakers' Union HQ. He also had influence with the AEU, the fitter's craft union. The diesel locomotives needed electricians but we had none. So Groom proposed that Boilermakers, as Craftsmen, could be trained as Electricians. I agreed; he called a vast meeting that lunchtime, there was unanimous agreement and without authority from Head of Personnel on the Eastern Region on my side or formal agreement from the Trade Unions on his, we went ahead. To put this through the 'proper channels' would have taken an eternity and those old Boilermakers made excellent electricians. My Lords and Masters found out what we had done about three months later but admitted that we had no alternative. How good it felt.

The inclusion of the *LNER Rulebook* gives me the opportunity to say what I have always felt strongly – that just like the enginemen in their private footplate, the signalman and the guard (freight or passenger) in charge of the train retained their own independence. All these men had to act without the orders of a boss, and each carried very real responsibility, playing his own part in the punctual running of the railway. Without doubt the signalman is the driver's best friend and any signalman who reads these words knows why. Indeed, I know this from my own experience. And so to Rule 55, which many will read with interest, noting its basic simplicity. The rule's application should be vital and immediate, but it can be neglected by signalman, guard, driver or fireman; it was that neglect that led to the appalling

Quintinshill disaster of 1915, the worst in the history of the railways of this country. I learned my own unforgettable lesson having run by a signal at danger in the blackout in 1943 through lack of attention. The time lost was regained and ranks were closed, with never a word said. But after that dark night up at Queensbury I never talked when signals at danger were in the offing; never, never again, nor when running into a terminus or up to and over a speed restriction.

Make the best of this section and enjoy the paragraphs on the use of the trolley – but remember, once on the track, he is as important as the most distinguished of passenger trains.

In 1949 E. A. Phillipson published a work of art entitled *The Steam Locomotive in Traffic*. I bought it soon after I took charge at Woodford Shed on the GC section in September 1949 – where the author had been Shedmaster in about 1936-7. He was greatly respected at Woodford, and this book is a testament to his expertise. How simple are the organisational charts of what is certainly the LNER Running Department. How clear and comprehensive he is when explaining technicalities and such rarely discussed subjects as coal handling, stores management and turntables, not to mention route knowledge. This was essential to the engine driver, as he was required to sign for the various routes, which meant that he had to know everything relevant to those stretches of line – track, signals, gradients, complexity of different routes, speed restrictions, stopping points at various stations; the list is endless. If you were to look at a railway map of Kent of the period, with East Surrey thrown in, you would see just how many routes there were from London Victoria to Dover. Yet there were senior men who had left school at 12 or 13 who signed for the whole of Kent, who knew the roads blindfold and who could work any train anywhere.

Somehow the great majority of our staff at Stewarts Lane in Battersea came to work punctually at all hours throughout the ghastly Great London Smog of December 1952, when you could barely see a couple of yards in front of you. And still the engines rolled off the shed to time, night and day, with enginemen prepared to work passenger trains under utterly desperate conditions until they got out into the country where the sky was blue and the sun shone. After it was all over, I chanced upon Driver Jimmy Nunn in the yard, a man who suffered very badly with his chest. I said to him, 'You did well to come to work in that lot, Jim' and his reply I shall never forget: 'Guv'nor, it was my duty to come to work'. I was mighty proud to know such men.

Phillipson does not mention the great advantages of the manning of engines where two or sometimes three sets of enginemen were booked to their own engine – the glory of polished copper, steel and brass on the footplate, the perfect movement of the engine, the economy of coal, oil and water, the understanding between men and machine and the resultant pride in the job. We had it all over the Eastern Region, even in the war at such a shed as Cambridge and later on wherever you went in our Stratford District on passenger engines almost up to the last days of steam in 1962.

The final extract comes from *The Locomotiveman's Pocket Book*. I remember buying this little booklet, which tells the fireman of the 1930s and '40s how to fire, how to use a shovel and how to build up a fire ready for a tough job. These are the basics and the drawings of good and bad fires certainly make the point; but they also beg a few questions. Diagram 1 shows the perfect fire for a gently sloping grate and no doubt with good coal. He will fire to a system, that is slightly heavier at the back than the sides and front corners, and will set his injector to feed water into the boiler so that the level remains constant and they will go mile after mile with the fireman firing maybe six shovels-full, no more, until the chimney is almost clear of smoke. But look at the drawing of Grosvenor's firebox and the acute slope of the grate and work out what would happen to that relatively thin fire under the firehole on Diagram 1. It would be dragged up to the front by the blast and heaped against the tubeplate and back would go the steam pressure. There are many classes of engine with such grates and you must keep the back end of the fire right up to the level of the top of the firehole door. Do this on a Southern Schools class or on a Great Central Director and you will have all the steam you want, but once that back end has got carted up to the front of the firebox, you are in deep trouble as in Diagram 4. We had 915 'Brighton' at Stewarts Lane: one Saturday she was in terrible trouble all the way to Newhaven after the fireman had lost control of his fire going up Grosvenor Road bank. The next day 915 went to Dover with a relief boat train, with the fire banked right up, indeed blacked out but with the firehole door open throughout. An experienced and thinking fireman is an artist with the shovel.

I will finish with the words of one of my heroes, J. G. Robinson of the Great Central Railway. I fired many miles on his engines and worked on them in the shed, and thought they were marvellous. During the Second World War it was always said that his 'RODs' had won the last war and would certainly help to do the same this time. I wrote to him accordingly and in due course, despite being by that time a very old man, who had reached the summit of his profession, he had the courtesy to reply to a young apprentice. He finished his letter by saying: 'Young man, never forget that there is no end to what you can learn about life and work on the railway.' How very true. I hope that you will enjoy and profit from reading these pages, for they are packed with practical and essential information which will give the reader a true feeling of what it was like to be a disciplined yet courageous Railwayman in years gone by.

R. H. N. Hardy
April 2011

BIOGRAPHY

Richard Harry Norman Hardy was born 8 October 1923 and attended Marlborough College before serving an apprenticeship at Doncaster Locomotive Works and Running Shed between 1941 and 1944. Here he obtained extensive footplate experience on all classes of LNER, GC and GN engines, covering some 60,000 miles. From there he moved to become Supernumerary Foreman at King's Lynn and South Lynn where he learnt all aspects of a Shedmaster's responsibility. He also acted in a relief capacity as a running foreman and Shedmaster at King's Lynn as well as Bury St Edmunds. He was involved in the installation and operation of pre-steaming apparatus at March, Cambs, in 1947, and the operation of the only oil-burner on the LNER; Eng 3152 class WD operating between Whitemoor and Temple Mills. From 1949 onwards he was appointed Shedmaster at Woodford Halse, moved to Ipswich in 1950 and then to Stewarts Lane, Battersea in 1952.

In 1955 he was promoted to Assistant District Motive Power Superintendent at Stratford and then in 1959 was appointed District Motive Power Superintendent at Liverpool St station at the time of the changeover from steam to diesel and electric traction. From 1963–June 1964 he was Acting Traffic Manager at Lincoln and then became Divisional Manager, King's Cross between 1964 and 1968, before moving to become Divisional Manager Liverpool (London Midland Region) between 1968 and 1973.

Richard's last job on the railways before retiring was Personnel Development Adviser (Engineering and Research), where he was responsible for the career development and appointments of professional engineers in all departments, from first appointments to Heads of Department and Engineers and in General Management. He retired from the railways in December 1982.

PREFACE

(Taken from 'The Locomotive Engineman's and Fireman's Examination Guide' 1893)

THE Author has had the pleasure of presiding over, and conducting during the past two years, a Mutual Improvement Class, which was formed for the especial purpose of training our junior foot-plate workers. The subjects we have studied include all conceivable kinds of failures of locomotives, and the best and most expeditious modes of dealing with them. How to test for Broken Valve Laps, Broken Ports, Pistons, Valves, etc.; Lap and Lead, and their use; Failures of Vacuum and Steam Brakes, and how to deal with them. And also what is of great importance, inasmuch as it facilitates the locating of the Cranks, Valves, &c.–How to read the locomotive. In other words, to obtain a view of one side rod, or one crank, and from that to be able to state with clearness and precision the exact position of every part of the Engine which gives motion to, or receives motion from, the crank shaft. Side rods, cranks, small ends, pistons, valves, eccentrics, and even the quadrant links can have their position indicated by those who have a practical acquaintance with the system adopted by the Author when engaged in the work of teaching. It is simple, therefore readily understood, and is worthy of a trial by those whose duties compel them to master the principles of locomotive construction.

The class of Engine chosen for the purpose of illustration may be described as follows: Six-wheeled-coupled, inside cylinders, piston stroke twenty-four inches, and Stephenson's link motion with open eccentric rods.

The Author has had the great pleasure of congratulating many young men on their passing a rather severe examination on the Locomotive, and has on such occasions received their thanks and a warm tribute to the methods adopted in our class and set forth in this book.

The leading features of the system here adopted to impress upon the memory the relative positions of the side rods, cranks, pistons, and valves, have never appeared in print before.

No doubt there are many enginemen more or less conversant with these positions, but to make them available for teaching the younger members of the foot-plate fraternity they needed arranging in proper order, or in other words, they wanted systemizing. This is what has been done. Chaos has been reduced to order, and the

result is a progressive system, easily learned, and as easily retained by the memory.

The side rod is taken as a starting point, from there to the crank is an easy step, it being opposite to it. It is only necessary to remember that the left-hand crank is one quarter behind the right-hand, to find it; and the left-hand side rod may be located in the same way by remembering that it is one quarter behind the right-hand side rod, or, on opposite quarters to the left-hand big end.

In this simple way, i.e., by knowing, and remembering, the exact relation which one part bears to another, and the advance which one part has of another, the whole of the movable parts of a locomotive may be located, or their position known if one part alone can be seen.

Trusting that this little work will prove useful and acceptable to the whole of the foot-plate fraternity, and hoping my critics will not be too severe, but remember that it is the offspring of a Driver desirous of benefiting his fellows,

I remain,
Yours very truly,
MAURICE G. VAUGHAN.
Plymouth, 1893.

Link Motions.

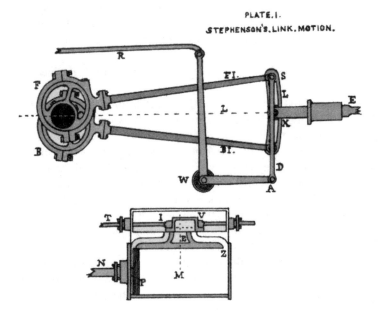

PLATE. I.

STEPHENSON'S. LINK. MOTION.

The majority of enginemen and firemen are interested in link motions; we illustrate two different kinds. Stevenson's and Allan's are common enough in this country.

C is the crank, F the fore gear eccentric and F1 its rod coupled to the top of the expansion link L. The back gear eccentric is shewn at B, and its rod B1 is attached to the bottom of the link L, and when arranged in this way the rods are said to be open and the motion direct. F is keyed on the axle in advance of the crank C when moving forward, and B is in advance of C when moving backward. This advance may be regarded as three distinct steps. The first brings the valve into position for admitting steam to the piston as soon as the crank moves if no lap or lead is given, as shewn by Figs. 14 and 14a, and is equal to one quarter of the axle circumference: The second and third advances bring the valve into position when lap and lead are added to the valve as Figs. 15 and 15a, and is termed the angular advance.

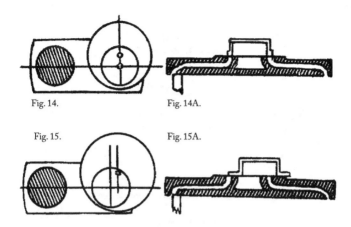

Fig. 14.   Fig. 14A.

Fig. 15.   Fig. 15A.

F and B are on a different centre to that of the axle, and the distance between these centres is termed the eccentricity, which is half the throw of the eccentrics, so that if the throw is four and a half inches the eccentricity is two and a quarter inches.

A fact to be remembered in connection with this motion is, the lead increases as the lever is notched up with open rods, and decreases with crossed rods, (Plate 2 shews the rods crossed) and the motion is indirect. R is the bridle rod leading to reversing lever, W the balance spring, A is the bottom of the lifting arm which is coupled to D the lifting link, this is coupled to the link at S which is the point of suspension, but it may be suspended at its middle as in plate 3, or at the bottom.

The link is curved to a radius equal to that of the eccentric rod.

In a curved slot in the link L, is the quadrant block X, from which extends the valve rod E, and the spindle T which passes into the steam chest and by means of a strap I holds the valve V in position, and moves it to fro when set in motion. N is piston rod, P the piston, E the exhaust port, Z the steam ports, and M the cylinder. As shewn in the figure the lever is in the centre notch, and if the axle be turned round both the eccentrics would actuate the valve. If the lever is put in fore gear S will descend to X, and the valve will be driven from that point principally by the eccentric F; if backward the bottom of the link will ascend to X, and the valve will be actuated from that

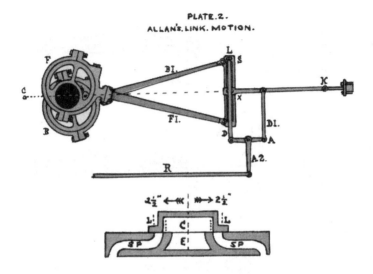

PLATE. 2.

ALLAN'S. LINK. MOTION.

point principally by the eccentric B. If the axle is moved a turn the link will receive two motions, one an oscillating and the other a reciprocating movement.

The first rocks the link to and from as though it were suspended at its centre on a fixed pivot, and the second carries it bodily to and fro on the line of motion.

We will first trace the origin of the reciprocating movement:

Fig. 16 shows us the position of the link when the crank C is on the back quarter, and the eccentrics in front of the axle, and the lever out of gear. X is the quadrant block, M the middle of valve travel, and F is the middle of the valve which is open to the lead at the back port as in plate 1. If we turn the axle round until the crank C is on the front quarter the eccentrics will be behind the axle as in Fig. 17, and the middle of valve F has been drawn from the front of M to the rear of it, and the valve is open to the lead at the front port. This change in the position of the valve is due then simply to the eccentric centres moving from the front to the back of the axle. And the link is pushed forward and pulled backward in a straight line a distance which is equal to the lap and lead of the valve.

Fig. 16.

Fig. 17.

Fig. 18.

Fig. 19.

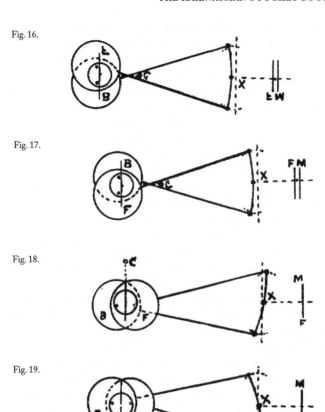

The oscillating motion is imparted to the link by the eccentrics revolving round the axle and in turn pulling and pushing the top and bottom of the link. We will move the crank one quarter from the position assigned it in the plate, now we find the top of the link has been pushed forward by the fore gear eccentric, whilst the bottom has been pulled backward by the back gear one as in Fig. 18, and the valve has been pulled to its mid travel as shewn by the lines M and F being joined together. Now we move the crank on to the bottom quarter as in Fig. 19, and whilst doing so we observe that the fore gear eccentric F has pulled back the top of link, and the back gear one has pushed fore the bottom of it, and thus the link is rocked to and fro; but the valve has not participated in this rocking motion as the block X is at the middle or dead point of the link, and it has simply oscillated as it would if X were a fixed point; but owing to the centres of the eccentrics being first in advance of the axle centre and then behind it, the valve has moved a distance equal to the measurement between these centres, backward and forward. Had the lever been put in forward gear then the top of the link would have dropped to X, and the valve would have received the full travel of the link, and the block X instead of being on the dotted line at Figs. 18 and 19 would have been in line with the top of the dark line representing the link, and the valve would then receive the full travel of the oscillating and to and fro movement.

We cannot do more in the available space than note the general arrangement and the points wherein this motion differs from Stevenson's, but sufficient is said to enable anyone to intelligibly discuss it.

The crank eccentrics and rods together with the reference letters are as in Plate 1, excepting the fact that the rods are crossed and the fore gear eccentric is coupled to the bottom of the link L. The link slot is straight, Stevenson's is curved. There are also two lifting links D and D1, D is attached to the top of the link at S. D1 is coupled to the valve rod and block X. R is the bridle rod leading to reversing lever, also to the bell crank A2. If the lever is put in forward gear the rod R and arm A2 move towards the fire box, and the arm A and hanger D1 descends whilst the link D ascends and pushes up the link. Thus we see that in Stevenson's motion the link only moves up or down, in Allan's the link ascends whilst the block and valve rod descends.

With this motion it is generally found to be a good plan in case of uncoupling to sever the connection with the valve at the joint K, and tie up the rod above the line of motion.

PREFACE

(Taken from 'Locomotive Engine Driving: A Practical Manual for Engineers in charge of locomotive engines' by Michael Reynolds, first published in 1877, with some text taken from the 1901 edition.)

I am ambitious to extend and improve the social condition of locomotive drivers by placing within their reach a standard test of capacity that will be unaffected by local or temporary prejudices, fancies, fashions, or accidental connections.

It appears to me that our enginemen of to-day will be to those of the next century what "Puffing Billy" in 1825 is to the "Monarch of Speed" in 1877. I hold a very strong opinion that our enginemen may be stripped of old habits and customs by self-help and self-reliance, and developed into a high state of efficiency. In carrying out such a measure of progress, difficulties, no doubt, which usually attend the work of reformation, will crop up; and many disappointments await the pioneer. The engine is ahead of the engineman—all the hard scheming, comparatively speaking, is done; but the engineman remains where he was in George Stephenson's time, and his stationary condition jars with his surroundings.

I propose to introduce certificates for locomotive drivers, which will in my opinion be an efficacious method of celebrating and crowning the great and mighty work of Stephenson, who particularly watched over the craft (enginemen), and was, I am informed, in his element when he was with them. One can easily understand this, for he was himself originally an engine-driver.

By means of certificates of proficiency I hope to see the vocation of engine-driver brought up to the standard of what, I think, Stephenson would have worked it to, had he lived longer. He would have made every possible provision for the recognition of ability, and for giving enginemen a fair opportunity of advancing with the engine and with the times. By such means each man would develop the brightest tints of his nature; and I see no reason why such anticipations should not come to maturity in the region of fact.

The life of engine-driving has in recent years undergone great changes for the better. In the improvements of engines and in personal comforts, introduced even during the last twenty years, locomotive enginemen may find much upon which to congratulate themselves. But–to summarise their experience–it has consisted of labour and bustle without progress. This unsatisfactory condition of things may, it is anticipated, be amended by the institution of certificates, with the encouragement of corresponding degrees of rank and of special uniforms. Certificates of examination afford a useful means of gauging a man's capacity, when one might otherwise be deceived by appearances.

My object in writing this work has been to communicate that species of knowledge which it is necessary for an engine-driver to possess who aspires to take high rank on the footplate, and to win a certificate of the first class. In the first part the elements of the locomotive are described, the general working conditions are specified, the principles and methods of inspection are elaborately set forth, and the causes of failure are analyzed and exposed. Moreover, the various duties of an engine-driver, from the moment that he enters the running-shed until he returns to it, are completely but concisely explained; whilst the duties and the training of a fireman are described with much detail, and the principles of the management of the fire–not an easy problem–are very fully investigated.

With a brief notice of the arithmetical problems which most usually come within the range of an engine-driver's practice, the scientific principles of expansion, combustion, &c., involved in his practice, are explained.

Finally, the groundwork of examination for first class, second-class, and third-class certificates of proficiency is succinctly set forth; to which is added a carefully compiled collection of regulations for enginemen and firemen.

Michael Reynolds

Fig.6 – Mr. WILLIAM STROUDLEY'S Locomotive "Grovesnor," London, Brighton, and South Coast Railway. Longitudinal Elevation

1.
2. } Barrel of boiler
3.
6. Smoke-box

22. Chimney
32. Spring balance
33. Whistle
34. Dome

64. Exhaust-pipe
70. Cab
85. Brake-blocks
87. Life-guards

88. Trailing-axle and wheel
89. Leading ditto
(54. Driving-axle)

O. Speed-indicator
P. Splasher
S. Sand-box
T. Tool ditto
V. Safety-valve

W. Balance in driving-wheel

Fig 6 a. "GROSVENOR"
Longitudinal Section

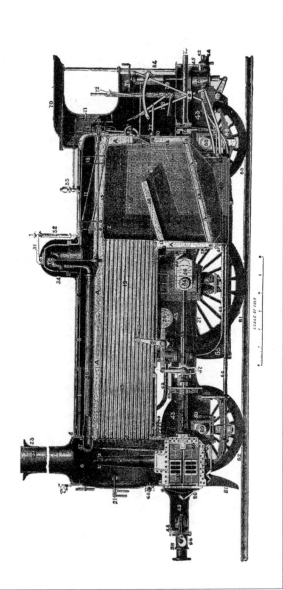

SCALE OF FEET

Longitudinal Section Key Fig 6a

1. ⎫ Rings arranged telescopically,
2. ⎬ forming barrel of
3. ⎭ boiler
4. Solid angle-iron ring
5. Tube-plate
6. Smoke-box
7. Shell, or covering-plate
8. Foundation-ring
9. Throat-plate
10. Back-plate
11. Fire-door
12. Covering-plate of inside fire-box
13. Tube-plate
14. Back-plate
15. Stays
16. Mouthpiece
17. Stays from inside firebox to shell-plate
18. Palm-stays
19. Tubes
20. Smoke-box door
21. Pinching-screw
22. Chimney
23. Chimney-cap
24. Blast-pipe
25. Top of blast-pipe
26. Balance-weight
27. Wheel-spokes
28. Front buffer
29. Mud-plug
30. Safety-valve
31. Ditto   lever
32. Spring balance
33. Whistle
34. Dome
35. Regulator
36. Steam-pipes
37. Elbow-pipe
38. Brick arch
39. Fire-bars
40. Ash-pan
41. Front damper
42. Back   ditto
43. Frame-plate
44. Iron buffer-beam (front)
45. Ditto   ditto (back)
46. See plan (cylinder)
47. Cylinder, ports, valve
48. Valve-chest
49. Steel motion-plate
50. Horn blocks
51. Axle-boxes
52. Slide-bars
53. Connecting-rod
54. Crank-shaft
55. Big end
56. Arm of ditto
57. Expansion-link
58. Weigh-bar shaft
59. Valve-spindle
60. Ditto   rod-guide (see plan)
61. Pump
62. Delivery-pipe
63. Feed ditto
64. Exhaust ditto
65. Volute spring
66. Draw-bar hook
67. Lamp-iron
68. Oil-cup
69. Ditto pipes
70. Cab
71. Regulator handle
72. Reversing-lever
73. Draw-bar
74. Ditto   pin
75. Steam-brake cylinder
76. Hand-brake
77. Sand-rod
78. Front damper
79. Back   ditto
80. Trailing-wheel
81. Driving   ditto
82. Leading-wheel
83. Spring
84. Hand-rail
85. Brake-blocks
86. Waste water-cocks
87. Life-guard
88. Trailing-axle
89. Leading   ditto
Z. Lead-plug

Fig. 6 b. "GROVESNOR"
Half-width Plan

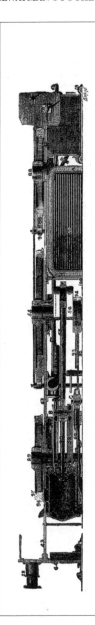

Half-width Plan

43. Frame-plate from end to end of engine
44. Iron buffer-beam
46. Cylinders
50. Horn block, to carry axle-box and brass
51. Axle-box and brass
52. Slide-bars
53. Connecting-rod
54. Driving-axle
55. Big end
56. Arm of ditto
59. Valve-spindle
60. Valve-rod guide
61. Pump
76. Hand-brake
85. Brake-blocks
88. Trailing-axle
89. Leading-axle
90. Piston-rod
91. Ditto head, held on the rod by a brass nut
92. Back-way ecc-rod
93. Front   ditto
94. Ecc-strap
95. Ecc-sheaves
96. Tyre
97. Lip on tyre
98. Brake-irons
99. Foot-plating
100. Transverse-stay
A. Water-space between inside and outside fire-boxes
B. Slide-block, with end of pump-ram screwed into the end
C. Link-motion (see 57 long. sec.)
D. Slide-valve-rod working-guide
H. Inside journal, showing the axle is supported inside of frame- plates
I. Cross-head, solid, with piston-rod

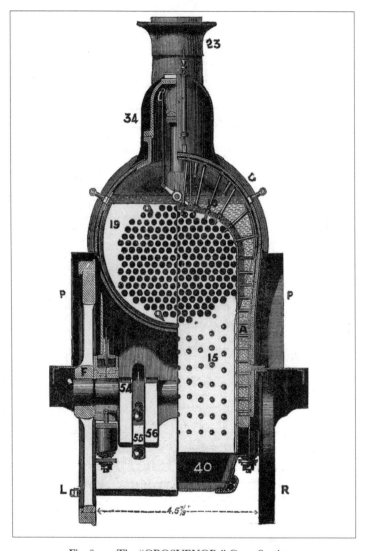

Fig. 6 c. – The "GROSVENOR." Cross Sections.

15. Stays in walls of fireboxes. 18. Ditto from crown-plate to covering-plate. 19. Tubes.
23. Chimney-cap. 40. Ash-pan. 54. Crank-shaft. 55. Big end. 56. Arm of big end. 34. Dome.
A. Water space. F. Nave of wheel. P.P. Splashers over driving-wheels. R. Right side of engine.
L. Left ditto.

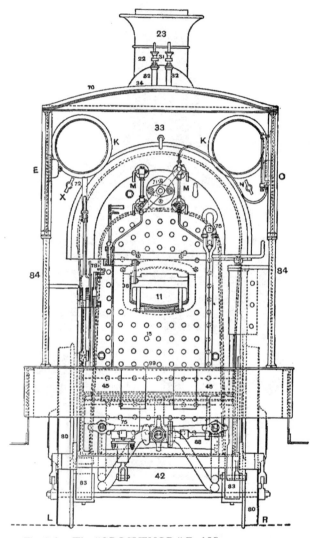

Fig. 6 d. – The "GROSVENOR." End View.

75. Steam-brake handle. 33. Whistle-handle. 23. Chimney-cap.K.K. Weather-glasses. O. Speed-indicator. E. Guard's bell. N. Oil for cylinder. X. Blower-handle. R. Right side of engine.

CERTIFICATES FOR DRIVERS AND FIREMEN

CERTIFICATES FOR LOCOMOTIVE DRIVERS

THE proposal to establish a system of certificates for locomotive drivers has been ventilated in the columns of *The Engineer*, and their universal adoption has been strongly recommended by the editor.

Enginemen would not only be improved by certificates, exciting a just and honest pride, but certificates would, as symbols of service and of competency, give much satisfaction.

The Engineer is of the opinion that, "In the first place, certificates would enable locomotive superintendents to form an excellent opinion as to the capacity, which is a different thing from the capabilities, of a man presenting himself for a berth; and in the second place, they would tend to elevate the position of, on the whole, an honest, trustworthy, and hardworking body of men. Certificates would supply the men with a stimulus to exertion; for they would enable the best men to come to the front and take the position which they desired; and the elevation of the type could scarcely fail to prove serviceable not only to the public but to railway companies."

The author is of opinion that every driver, before he is permitted to take charge of the regulator, should serve as a fireman on goods and passenger trains not less than 150,000 miles, after which he may offer to pass an examination, and obtain, if possible, a third-class certificate, and hold himself in readiness for an engine. This certificate might read as follows:–

Third-class Locomotive Driver's Certificate
"This is to certify that J. Stubbs has served as a fireman on goods and passenger engines 150,000 miles or upwards, that he has passed a third-class examination, and is a competent person to take charge of a locomotive engine working goods trains."

The subjects on which examination should be made, to obtain this certificate, should embrace reading, writing, signals, examination of engines before joining the trains, firing, trimming of siphons, oiling, testing of valves and pistons, and the various modes of uncoupling engines when they fail with a train. After having run 100,000 miles as a driver, and gained confidence and experience, a third-class engineman should be at liberty to apply for a second-class certificate, which might read thus:–

Second-class Locomotive Driver's Certificate
"This is to certify that N. Forster has served as a driver 100,000 miles on goods and passenger trains, that he has passed a second-class examination, and is a competent person to take charge of a locomotive engine working passenger trains."

The subjects to be questioned upon for this certificate might be printed on a form, so that they could be obtained at any time; and they should embrace the steam-engine and boiler described generally, combustion considered practically, steam, and the principle of its expansion. After having run with this certificate 50,000 miles, a driver might be entitled to apply for a first-class certificate, which might read:–

First-class Locomotive Engineer's Certificate
"This is to certify that E. Sparrow has served as a driver 150,000 miles, that he has passed a third-class, second-class, and first-class examination, and is a competent driver to take charge of a locomotive engine working express trains."

The subjects to be questioned on to obtain this certificate should be printed on forms and marked, "Subject 1," "Subject 2," &c., &c., which should embrace–1st, diagram of the applicant's engine-running; 2nd, drawing of elementary forms; 3rd, working drawing, with dimensions of any part of a locomotive engine; 4th, arithmetic, decimals, mensuration of superficies and solids; 5th, natural science, mechanics to explain the safety-valve lever, hydraulics to explain the pump, hydrostatics to explain the water in the gauge-glass, pneumatics to explain the pet-cock; 6th, chemistry, caloric to explain heat and expansion, oxygen to explain combustion, composition of coal to give the percentage of carbon, hydrogen, oxygen, nitrogen, sulphur, and ash, composition of water to give the percentage of oxygen and hydrogen.

The subjects above specified embrace nearly all that a locomotive driver need be expected to know to obtain a certificate; and, as the author is of opinion that the time is at hand when such tokens of capacity will be in vogue everywhere, he has noticed each subject, and given some examples in arithmetic, &c., &c., with rules for the benefit of those whose early education was *nil*, but who are ambitious to reach a locomotive driver's certificate.

Some such evidence should be produced by every locomotive foreman. The foreman should also have certificates of competency as well as the men.

REGULATIONS FOR ENGINEMEN AND FIREMEN.

CODE OF SIGNALS.

As the *Public Safety* is the first care of every officer and servant of a Railway Company, and is chiefly dependent upon the proper use and observance of the *Signals*, *all persons* employed are particularly *required* to make themselves *familiar with this code*.

The Signals in regular use are:

SEMAPHORES...............}   by *Day.*
FLAGS.........................}
LAMPS........................   by *Night.*

Also, PERCUSSION and PERSONAL SIGNALS.
Flags and Lamps are distinguished by Colours, as follows:
RED is a Signal of *Danger – Stop.*
GREEN – Caution–Proceed Slowly.
WHITE – All right – Go on.

HAND SIGNALS.

Men required to give Hand Signals are provided with Red, Green, and White Flags, and a Signal Lamp, with Red, Green, and White Glasses, and with Fog Signals; but in any emergency, when not provided with those means of signalling, the following are adopted, namely.

The ALL RIGHT SIGNAL is shown by extending the arm horizontally, so as to be distinctly seen by the Engine-driver, thus: (Fig. 24).

Fig. 24.

The CAUTION SIGNAL, to Proceed Slowly, is shown by one arm held straight up, thus: (Fig. 25).

Fig. 25.

The STOP SIGNAL is shown by holding both arms straight up, thus, or by waving any object with violence. (Fig. 26).

Fig. 26.

STATIONARY (SEMAPHORE) SIGNALS

Semaphore Signals are constructed with Arms for day Signals, and Coloured Lamps for night and foggy weather.

The "Danger Signal" is shown, in the day time, by the arm on the left-hand side of the post being raised to the horizontal position, thus: (Fig. 27).

and by the exhibition of a *red* light at night.

Fig. 27.

The "Caution Signal" is shown, in the day time, by the arm on the left-hand side of the post being placed half-way to the horizontal position, thus: (Fig. 28).

and by the exhibition of a *green* light at night.

Fig. 28.

The "All Right Signal" is shown, in the day time, by the left-hand side of the post being clear, thus: (Fig. 29).

and by a *white* light at night.

Fig. 29.

PERCUSSION OR FOG SIGNALS.

The *Percussion Signal* is used in addition to the ordinary Day and Night Signals in *foggy weather*, and when *unforeseen obstructions* have occurred which render it necessary to *stop* approaching trains.

It is fixed upon the rail (label upwards) by bending down the leaden clips attached to it for that purpose, and upon being run over by an engine or train *explodes* with a loud report.

The Signal, *Caution–Proceed slowly*, after bringing the train to a stand, is to be given by the explosion of one Fog Signal.

The Signal, *Danger–Stop*, is to be given by the *explosion* of *two* or *more* Fog Signals in near succession.

HAND SIGNALS BY NIGHT.

To *prevent* ordinary *Hand Lamps* being *mistaken for Signals*, men must avoid waving them when moving about, unless when absolutely necessary, taking care in all cases to hold the *dark side* as much as possible towards the *Engine-driver*. In the exhibition of *Hand Signals*, men on duty should select positions *conspicuous* to the Enginemen and Guards of Trains.

To provide for the proper guidance of the movement of trains *taking on* or *putting off* Waggons or Carriages upon some railways at *Stations*, the following Signals are used:-

When the Train at a Station is wanted to be moved *forward* to the points of a Connection or Siding, the *Guard, when on the ground*, signals to the Engineman for this by moving his *Green Light up and down*, and continues to do so until the tail of the train is far enough forward, when he gives a *Signal to Stop*, by showing a *Red Light*.

When the train has to be *backed* through a Connection or into a Siding, the Guard moves his *Green Light from side to side* across his body, and continues to do so until the train is far enough through, when he stops the train by exhibiting a *Red Light*.

Again, when the train has to return to the Main Line, the Guard signals with his *White Light* by moving it *from side to side* across his body, continuing to do so until the Train arrives on the Main Line. When he takes his place on the Train he signals to the Engineman to proceed on his journey by simply showing a *White Light*.

During these movements all parties are required to see that a *proper look-out* is kept, to prevent collisions with other Trains coming up, and each, in his department, to take the necessary precautions.

BEFORE STARTING.

The enginemen and firemen should appear on duty as clean as circumstances will allow; and they should be with their engines at such time previous to starting as their foreman may require, in order to see that the engines are in proper order to go out.

Every engineman, before starting his day's work, is in all cases to *inspect the notices* affixed to the noticeboards in the steam-sheds, in order to ascertain if there is anything requiring his special attention on parts of the line over which he is going to work, as he is responsible for any accident that may take place owing to his neglecting to read the notices posted in the sheds.

The duty of each engine-driver is determined by the locomotive superintendent; and no turn of duty should be altered, and no over-work should be undertaken, by any man, on any account, without the sanction of the locomotive superintendent, or his foreman, except on sudden emergencies, and it must then be reported by the engine-driver in his daily return.

It is the duty of *drivers, before starting*, to see that their engines are in proper working order, have the necessary *supply of coal* and *water*, that the *fog-signals* are in a fit *state for use*, and that all the necessary *tools* and *stores* are on the tender, and in efficient order.

Enginemen should always see before starting that their lights are in proper order, and that they have the proper distinguishing light for the train they are drawing.

Under no pretence are enginemen allowed to meddle with safety-valves, to obtain higher steam pressure.

Snow brooms must not be used on the engine guard-irons except snow is actually on the ground, lest they should remove fog signals placed on the rails.

Enginemen when leaving the shed should test the pumps or injectors and sand-valves, to see they work properly; particular attention must also be given to those parts recently renewed, and should any irregularities be felt or heard, the engine must be stopped and examined.

No person, except the proper engineman and fireman, is allowed to ride on the engine or tender without the special permission of the directors, or one of the chief officers of the company; and no fireman must move an engine except when instructed by the driver, and unless he has also an order from the superintendent.

WHILST RUNNING.

Engine-drivers are strictly enjoined to start and stop their trains slowly and without a jerk, so as to avoid the risk of snapping the couplings; and, except in case of danger, they must be careful not to shut off steam suddenly, and thereby cause unnecessary concussion of carriages or waggons. On starting, the fireman must look out behind to see that all the carriages are attached and all right.

When two engines are employed in drawing the same train, the engineman of the second engine must watch for and take his signals from the engineman of the leading engine, and great caution must be used in starting such a train to prevent the breaking of the couplings.

Every engine-driver is provided with a time-table, showing the exact time in which each journey is to be performed, excepting for special and ballast trains, the speed of which must be regulated by circumstances. He must endeavour to run the engine at a uniform speed, from which he should vary as little as possible. He must on no account run before the time specified in the time-table: and he will do well to consult the following table frequently, to enable him to judge with certainty the rate at which he is travelling, or should travel, to arrive at a given station at a certain time.

Speed per hour.	Time of performing ¼ mile.	Time of performing ½ mile.	Time of performing 1 mile.	Speed per hour.	Time of performing ¼ mile.	Time of performing ½ mile.	Time of performing 1 mile.
Miles.	m. s.	m. s.	m. s.	Miles.	m. s.	m. s.	m. s.
5	3 0	6 0	12 0	33	0 27	0 54	1 49
6	2 30	5 0	10 0	34	0 26	0 53	1 46
7	2 8	4 17	8 34	35	0 25	0 51	1 43
8	1 52	3 45	7 30	36	0 25	0 50	1 40
9	1 40	3 20	6 40	37	0 24	0 48	1 37
10	1 30	3 0	6 0	38	0 23	0 47	1 34
11	1 21	2 43	5 27	39	0 23	0 46	1 32
12	1 15	2 30	5 0	40	0 22	0 45	1 30
13	1 9	2 18	4 37	41	0 21	0 43	1 27
14	1 4	2 8	4 17	42	0 21	0 42	1 25
15	1 0	2 0	4 0	43	0 20	0 41	1 23
16	0 56	1 52	3 45	44	0 20	0 40	1 21
17	0 53	1 46	3 31	45	0 20	0 40	1 20
18	0 50	1 40	3 20	46	0 19	0 39	1 18
19	0 47	1 34	3 9	47	0 19	0 38	1 16
20	0 45	1 30	3 0	48	0 18	0 37	1 15
21	0 42	1 25	2 51	49	0 18	0 36	1 13
22	0 40	1 21	2 43	50	0 18	0 36	1 12
23	0 39	1 18	2 36	51	0 17	0 35	1 10
24	0 37	1 15	2 30	52	0 17	0 34	1 9
25	0 36	1 12	2 24	53	0 17	0 34	1 7
26	0 34	1 9	2 18	54	0 16	0 33	1 6
27	0 33	1 6	2 13	55	0 16	0 32	1 5
28	0 32	1 4	2 8	56	0 16	0 32	1 4
29	0 31	1 2	2 4	57	0 15	0 31	1 3
30	0 30	1 0	2 0	58	0 15	0 31	1 2
31	0 29	0 58	1 56	59	0 15	0 30	1 1
32	0 28	0 56	1 52	60	0 15	0 30	1 0

TABLE showing the speed of an Engine, when the time of performing a Quarter, Half, or One Mile is given.

When an engine is in motion, the *driver* must stand where he can keep a *good look-out ahead.*

The fireman must also keep a sharp *look-out*, when not otherwise engaged, and especially for any *signals from the guard*, which he will immediately communicate to the engineman.

Firemen must always *obey the orders* of enginemen.

Enginemen should before starting ascertain the number of vehicles in their trains, in order to work their engines accordingly.

Enginemen should not close the regulator to cut the steam off with the reversing-gear, and they should allow their engines to get away smart, with a few vigorous beats, before pulling the lever up, which should be done by degrees as the speed increases.

Enginemen must pay *implicit attention* to the *orders and signals of guards* in all matters relating to the stopping or starting of trains.

Enginemen must on no account place any reliance on the belief that their train is signalled by telegraph; as the fact of a train being so signalled should not in any way diminish the vigilance of their "look-out."

The fixed station, junction, and distant signals, with the hand and detonating signals, must alone be regarded and depended on by the enginemen.

Enginemen and *firemen* must pay *immediate attention to all signals*, whether the *cause* of their being given is *known* to them *or not*.

On approaching junctions, enginemen are to sound the whistle, to give the pointsmen notice of their approach. Enginemen are, as far as practicable, to have their firemen disengaged when passing a station, or on approaching or passing a junction, so that they may assist to keep a good look-out for signals.

When an engineman finds a distant signal exhibiting the danger signal, he must immediately turn off steam, and reduce the speed of his train, *so as to be able to stop at the distant signal*; but if he sees that the way is clear he must proceed slowly and cautiously within the distant signal, having such control of his train as to be able to *stop it at any moment*, and bring his engine or train to a stand as near the station or junction as the circumstances will allow.

Whenever a distant or other signal appears in any intermediate position to the proper distances at which it works, it is to be treated as if indicating "Stop," the presumption being that the machinery of the signal is out of order.

The absence of a signal at a place where a signal is ordinarily shown, or a signal imperfectly exhibited, is to be considered as a danger signal, and treated accordingly.

Whenever an engineman *perceives a red flag, or other symbol*, which he understands to be a signal *to stop*, he must bring his engine to a *complete stand close to the signal*, and must on no account pass it.

An unlighted signal after dark must be considered a stop signal.

There may be cases requiring a train to stop, either from a signal or from the personal observation of the engine-driver, when the most prompt judgment and skill will be required to decide whether to stop quickly or merely to shut off the steam, and then let the train stop of itself; this must be left to the judgment of the driver. As a general rule, it may be considered that, if anything is the matter with the engine requiring to stop, the quicker it can be done the better; but if any intermediate parts of the train are off the rails, allowing the carriages to stop of themselves has, in some cases, kept up a disabled carriage, when it is probable, if the brake had been applied in front, the carriages behind would have forced themselves over the disabled one. If, however, the disabled carriage should be the last, or nearly the last, in the train, the brake in front may be applied with advantage; but if towards the middle or the front of the train, it is better to let the carriages stop gradually, as, by keeping up a gentle pull, the disabled carriage is kept more out of the way of those behind until the force of the latter is exhausted. In all cases the application of brakes behind the disabled carriages will be attended with the greatest advantage and safety.

The engine whistle must not be used more than is absolutely necessary, the sound being calculated to alarm and disturb passengers, and the public residing in the vicinity of the railway, and to frighten horses.

When two engines are with a train, the signals are to be made by the leading engine.

As a general rule, enginemen are at all times to exercise the greatest watchfulness; they are to be ever on the alert, and, while on duty, to keep their minds entirely fixed on that which is required to be done.

If an engineman should observe anything wrong on the line of rails opposite to that on which his train is running, or should he meet an engine or train too closely following any preceding engine or train, he must exhibit a caution or danger signal, as occasion may require, to the engineman of such following engine or train.

When the road is obscured by steam or smoke (owing to a burst tube or any other cause), no approaching engine is allowed to *pass through the steam* until the engineman shall have ascertained that the road is clear; and if any engineman perceive a train stopping, from accident or other cause, on the road, he is immediately to *slacken his speed*, so that he may pass such train slowly, and stop altogether if necessary, in order to ascertain the cause of the stoppage, and report it at the next station.

Where there is an accident on the opposite line to that on which he is moving, he is to stop all the trains between the spot and the next station, and caution the respective enginemen; and he is, further, to render every assistance in his power in all cases of difficulty.

Engine-drivers must report, immediately on arrival at the first station, any obstruction upon the line from slips or other causes.

When meeting another engine, the drivers should stand on the right-hand side, so as to be near each other in passing, ready to give or receive a signal whether the line which they have passed is clear, whether a train is a-head, or any cause of danger exists.

Enginemen, in bringing up their trains, are to pay particular attention to the state of the weather and the condition of the rails as well as to the length of the train; and these circumstances must have due weight in determining when to shut off the steam. Stations must not be entered so rapidly as to require a violent application of the breaks.

In going down inclined planes, enginemen must take care that they have complete control over the trains, by applying their breaks; and they must on no account attempt to make up lost time in going down inclined planes.

No train with two engines attached is to be allowed to descend any inclined plane without the steam being shut off the second engine.

Due regard must be paid to the caution boards passed at various parts of the line, and the drivers are strictly forbidden to exceed the speed marked thereon where it is specified.

Enginemen must carefully approach all stations at which their trains are required to stop, and must not overrun the platform.

In no case the engine-driver to put back when he has run past a station until he receives a signal from the station-master or guard; and he must be careful to avoid any delay from overrunning or stopping short of stations.

Enginemen are warned against improperly cottering up any joint or brass, and thereby causing the journals to become hot, or allowing any slide, block, or journal to cut or tear for want of oil or grease.

The fireman is to look back at starting from a station to see that the stop signal is not subsequently given, and that all the train is attached, and frequently when on the journey, and more particularly in passing all points where a signalman is stationed, to observe if he or the guard continues the "all right" signal after the train has passed, or turns on the "stop" signal to indicate that something is wrong, and to *satisfy himself* the engine is *on the right line*.

In case a train, when in motion, should become disconnected into two or more parts, care must be taken not to stop the front part of the train before the detached portions have either stopped or come gently up.

Should *fire* be discovered in a train, the steam must be instantly shut off, the brakes applied, and the train brought to a stand; the proper signals must then be made for the protection of the line, and the burning vehicle or vehicles be detached with as little delay as possible, and the best means adopted to extinguish the fire.

Whenever an engine passes over a detonating signal, or a hand signal to stop is seen, the driver must *immediately shut off steam*, and proceed with *great caution* until he has ascertained that the line is *quite clear*, or until a *second signal* is passed, when the train must be *stopped immediately*.

Should an accident occasion the stoppage of both lines of railway, the engineman must send the fireman in advance of the train to signal trains travelling on the opposite line of rail to that upon which his train was running.

The following is the mode of applying the detonating signals. In case of obstruction, where it is necessary to stop any engine or train following on the same line, one of the signals is to be placed by the person engaged in the duty, at the end of *every* 250 yards, for a distance of not less than 1,000 yards from the place of obstruction (on levels, but farther on descending gradients, or, if a curve, to continue it until the red signal can be seen round the curve; and should the distance end in a tunnel, then the signal is to be exhibited at the end of the tunnel furthest from the obstruction), in the proper direction, and *two* must be fixed *ten yards apart* at the point where the signalman stands at the moment a following train comes in sight, or, on arriving at the end of the distance named, between him and the approaching train: *five* signals will thus be required to protect the train. The *stop flag signal*, or *lamp at night*, must at the same time be exhibited as conspicuously as possible, and *every exertion* made to stop any approaching engine or train.

AT STATIONS AND STOPPING PLACES.

On stopping at a station, the engine-driver should examine and oil the engine, and if any of the journals or working parts are hot, they must have more oil, and, if necessary, be eased.

Whenever an engine is standing, the spare steam must be turned into the tender, so as to allow as little as possible to escape by the safety-valves.

In all cases when an engine is standing, however short the time, the tender-brake is to be screwed on tight until the signal is given for starting.

Enginemen and firemen must not go away from their engines during their hours of duty, unless authorised by the locomotive foreman, and must never leave an engine in steam without shutting the regulator, putting the engine out of gear, and fixing down the tender-brake.

Whenever an engine-driver is required by a stationmaster to do anything which may appear in excess of the driver's duty or unreasonable, he is not to refuse to do it unless inconsistent with safety; but the matter is to be referred to the locomotive superintendent.

Enginemen are not allowed (except in case of accident or sudden illness) to change their engines on the journey, nor to leave their respective stations without the permission of their superior officers.

It is very important that engine-drivers use the utmost caution when shunting waggons into sidings, so as to avoid injuring the waggons or other property of the Company.

Engine-drivers should avoid, as much as possible, blowing off steam or opening the feed-pipes at stations, or in passing trains or men, or anywhere where the steam might occasion danger by obstructing the sight.

Enginemen and firemen must not interfere with points connected with the main line except in cases of extreme urgency, and when there is no pointsman who can attend to them.

Every engine-driver is to afford all assistance with his engine that may be required for the arrangement and despatch of the trains; and if running an engine alone or with goods, he must not refuse loaded or empty waggons, if he has power to pull them, unless he has special orders on the subject.

If a train, or a portion of it, is drawn into a station or a siding with a tow-rope, care must be taken to stretch the rope gradually by a gentle advance of the engine; and great attention must be paid to the signals given by the man conducting the operation.

When trains are shunted for other trains to pass, the tail lamps must be removed, or so disposed as not to exhibit the red light to the following train.

AT THE END OF A JOURNEY.

The engine-driver after every trip should carefully examine his engine, test the valves and pistons, and make immediate report to the locomotive superintendent or foreman of any accident to it or to the train; as also of any obstruction or defect in the line, neglect of signals, or other irregularity observed during the journey.

Every engineman, at the conclusion of the day's work, must put his engine in the place appointed for it after the fireman has dropped the fire and raked the ash-pan clean out over the pit appropriated for that purpose; and he must see that the regulator is left properly shut, the engine out of gear, tender-brake on, and the boiler properly filled with water.

Every engineman, at the *end of his journey*, must report in the driver's report-book provided for that purpose—*first*, as to *the state of his engine* and tender; *second*, as to any defect in the road; third, as to any defect in the working of signals, as to any irregularity in the working of his trains, such as time lost by engine and traffic causes, hot axles, &c.

The engine-driver is to keep an account of the duty performed by his engine, and make a daily return of the same to the foreman.

❧

The Great Northern Railway

PRACTICAL QUESTIONS

FOR

DRIVERS AND FIREMEN.

LOCOMOTIVE DEPARTMENT,
DONCASTER,
January 1st, 1903.
DONCASTER:

R. H. HEPWORTH, BOROUGH PRINTING WORKS, 49, HIGH STREET. 1903.

I wrote this catechism almost in its present form in the year 1883, for the use of Drivers and Firemen on the Great Southern and Western Railway of Ireland. A few questions have been added or altered to bring it more up to date, it is intended to be of some assistance chiefly to the younger men. They will notice that the questions do not go into details regarding the construction of various engines, valve gears, or the action of the injector, or combustion of fuel, &c.; there are plenty of good books to be had describing all these. Any man who takes an interest in his work and wants to get on will read such books and attend instruction classes to obtain all the information he can so that he does not get left behind.

H. A. IVATT,

January 1st, 1903.

GETTING READY FOR A TRAIN

1.　　Q.–What is an engineman's first duty when coming to work?

　　A.–He should sign the "appearance" book and read the "notice" board.

2.　　Q.–What are the first things an engineman should see to on taking charge of his engine in the shed, before going out for his train?

　　A.–He should examine the water gauges to see that there is a proper quantity of water in the boiler, and to make sure that the gauges are working correctly, and not shewing false water. He should also see what pressure of steam there is, and notice the state of the fire and that the coal is properly stacked on the tender or bunker.

3.　　Q.–How do you make up a fire with Welsh coal?

　　A.– To make up a good fire for a long run with Welsh coal, it should be put on 1½ or even 2 hours before train time, as it takes a long time to burn through. It should be put on in lumps all round the walls of the box (if the lumps are large they can be put on by hand), and it should be thickest under the door and in the back corners. No coal should he put in the middle of the box unless the bars are bare.

4.　　Q.–Does the same rule apply to hard, or as it is sometimes called, "sharp" coal?

　　A.–Yes; except that this sort of coal burns more quickly than Welsh, and therefore need not be put on so long before train time.

5.　　Q.–Some sorts of coal form a hard and close clinker on the fire-bars; can anything be done by the fireman to improve matters when working with this sort of coal?

A.–Yes; a very good plan is to scatter some broken brick (old arch bricks) over the bars before making up the fire. The bricks should be broken up into pieces rather smaller than a man's fist. Broken limestone is also a good thing to use for this purpose, particularly with some sorts of coal.

6.   Q.–Having made up his fire, what should a fireman do next?

A.–He should clean up his foot-plate and boiler front, see that the sand-boxes are full, and that the sand gear will work, and that the sand is not damp, see that the head lamps are in proper order and in their right places.

ON THE ROAD

7.   Q.–What should a driver's first thought be when running?

A.–The safety of his train.

8.   Q.–In what condition should the engine be before starting with a train?

A.–The fire should be well burned through, the boiler moderately full of water, and the steam pressure near the blowing-off point and all bearings oiled.

9.   Q.–Do not some drivers fill up their boilers before starting till the water nearly comes out of the safety valves?

A.–Yes; some second class men do this; but it is a great mistake, because when the regulator is opened, the engine works the first few strokes with hot water instead of steam, and this takes all the lubrication off the valve faces and from the cylinders, making the engine work stiff, and preventing her from pulling what she would do if properly handled.

IN THE SHED

10.   Q.– What is meant in speaking of a right-hand crank engine, or a left-hand crank engine?

A.– A right hand crank engine is one in which the right crank leads, and a left-hand crank engine is one in which the left crank leads.

11.   Q.– What do you mean by the right crank leading, or the left crank leading?

A.– When the engine is standing with one crank on the back centre (that is, pointing towards the fire box) and the other on the top centre (that is, pointing towards the boiler), if the right crank comes on the top centre, the right crank leads; but if it is the left crank which is on the top centre, then the left crank leads.

12.   Q.– Looking at the left side of one of Mr Stirling's 8ft. engines, if the left big end is at the top, where is the other?

A.– On the front centre.

13.   Q.– How do you know that?

A.– Because the right crank leads on nearly all Great Northern engines, and the one that leads is always a quarter turn ahead of the other.

ENGINE BREAKDOWNS

14.   Q.– If an engine breaks down from any cause while running what should a driver do?

A.– He should stop and see what is wrong, and get the engine into working order, so as to take the train forward as quickly as possible. Where less delay will be caused by getting another engine, this should be done at once.

15.   Q.– Mention a few of the principal causes of engine failures on the road.

A.– Choked or dirty fire, leaking tubes or stays, burst tube, broken coupling rod, broken connecting rod, slack cotter in piston or valve spindle cross-heads, broken eccentric-rod, broken piston-rod, cotters working out of big end, or little end, motions pins working out; big or little end, or boxes running hot, broken tyre, broken crank axle.

16.   Q.– When from leaking or other cause the pressure falls fast enough to put the brake on and make the train pull hard, what is best to be done to get to a place where you can stand or change engines?

A.– The best way is to stop at once (under signals, if possible) and get the brake off the train; put the hand-brake on, and set the small ejector to blow about 10, or whatever the lower pressure of steam will hold, and let the fireman and the guard bleed the brakes off the coaches by pulling the wires. This will save time in the end by making the train easy to pull, and is better than struggling on with the blocks rubbing and no steam.

17.   Q.– When a tube bursts what is the right thing to do?

A.– Get it plugged as soon as possible. When the tube bursts, put on both ejectors, and if you can manage to get under the protection of signals before you stop, so much the better. The water will generally damp the fire sufficiently, but if the burst is near the smoke box, the bulk of the water may go that way, and the driver must be prepared to pull the fire back and damp it if necessary. If the burst is not a very bad one, the plugs can generally be got in before the steam pressure is all exhausted, and so leave something to blow up the fire, and save time after plugging.

SPEED TABLE.

To use this table, take the number of seconds occupied in running a quarter of a mile, look in the table for this figure and opposite to it (in the other column) will be found the speed in miles per hour.

Thus: if it takes 18 seconds to run a quarter mile, the speed is 50 miles per hour; or if it takes 50 seconds to run a quarter mile the speed is 18 miles per hour. A quarter mile in 10 seconds is 90 miles per hour; a quarter mile in 90 seconds is 10 miles per hour, and so on throughout the table.

90	10	50	18
$85\frac{3}{4}$	$10\frac{1}{2}$	$48\frac{2}{3}$	$18\frac{1}{2}$
$81\frac{3}{4}$	11	$47\frac{1}{3}$	19
$78\frac{1}{4}$	$11\frac{1}{2}$	$46\frac{1}{7}$	$19\frac{1}{2}$
75	12	45	20
72	$12\frac{1}{2}$	$42\frac{3}{4}$	21
$69\frac{1}{4}$	13	41	22
$66\frac{2}{3}$	$13\frac{1}{2}$	$39\frac{1}{7}$	23
$64\frac{1}{4}$	14	$37\frac{1}{2}$	24
62	$14\frac{1}{2}$	36	25
60	15	$34\frac{2}{3}$	26
58	$15\frac{1}{2}$	$33\frac{1}{3}$	27
$56\frac{1}{4}$	16	$32\frac{1}{7}$	28
$54\frac{1}{2}$	$16\frac{1}{2}$	31	29
53	17	30	30
$51\frac{2}{5}$	$17\frac{1}{2}$		

NOTES ON NEW PASSENGER COMMUNICATION

Carriages are now being fitted with a new form of Passenger communication.

When a passenger pulls the communication chain inside the carriage, it springs a leak in the brake pipe and applies the brake. The application is not so quick as to stop the train at once, but the driver can, by means of the large ejector, hold the brake off long enough to get clear of a tunnel or other bad place for stopping, if necessary. The vacuum gauge begins to fall and the brake to go on slowly as soon as the passenger communication is pulled. When this happens the driver should stop at once, and send his mate back to tell the guard.

The hole in the brake pipe cannot be closed until the guard re-sets the apparatus.

NOTES ON WATER SCOOP TENDERS

The speed when putting in the scoop to pick up water must not exceed 50 miles an hour.

The water will go into the tender when the speed is about 20 miles an hour, and no more will be picked up at 50 miles an hour than at 25 or 30, but rather less, because at the higher speed the water heaps up at the back of the tank and overflows before it has time to settle down level.

Drivers working scoops which are lifted by the vacuum should leave the handle in the "out" position for a minute or so after taking water, to make certain that the scoop is well up before the lever is put into the middle or "running" position.

Drivers should examine and try the working of the scoop when over the pit before each trip to see that it is working all right. Any damage to the nose of the scoop, or any sign of the cutting edge being pulled down should be reported at once.

In frosty weather, particularly at night, if there is any doubt about the water being frozen, don't use the scoop, but stop and take water at the most convenient station.

Note.–A carriage has been thrown off the road at water-troughs by using the scoop when there was too much ice on the water, the ice piled up in front of the scoop until the heap was too big for the coaches to clear.

Drivers should be careful not to lower the scoop until they get on the end of the trough. When it is too dark to see the water, opening the fire door a little will give enough light to catch the white mark board, fixed at the commencement of the trough.

Doubling the speed more than doubles the pressure of the water on the nose of the scoop, in fact makes it four times as much. At 30 miles an hour the pressure on the scoop when in the water is about 5-cwts., at 60 miles an hour the pressure is four times as great, or about 20 cwts.

LOCOMOTIVE MANAGEMENT,

FROM

CLEANING TO DRIVING

(Taken from 'Locomotive Management from Cleaning to Driving, 1909')

FROM CLEANING TO DRIVING may often appear a long, and many times a thorny path, to the rising fireman or cleaner, ere the responsible position of locomotive driver is attained.

It may be taken that the young man, whose ambition is to be some day the driver of an express passenger train, will have already satisfied the locomotive superintendent or shed foreman as to his credentials and that he has satisfactorily passed through the height and sight tests.

COMMENCING AS A CLEANER the young man will in many sheds be first given the tender wheels to operate on. After about three months, promotion to tender tank and framing should take place, until the further advancement to cleaning of the engine is merited.

It is during this engine cleaning period that the foundation of the future driver's career is laid. To be smart, civil and obliging, and to have his engine spotlessly clean are the very best of recommendations.

THE BOILER AND TANK should be washed with a little soap and water at least once a week.

So as to be in readiness for the time when he is called upon as a spare fireman, the cleaner should be taught to take notice how the fireman makes up his fire, and should be trained to make himself thoroughly acquainted with the different classes of oil cans, tools, fire-irons, &c., and to give a helping hand to either driver or fireman if required, paying particular attention at the same time to the screwing up or packing of glands.

Among other things the cleaner should watch the washer-out, the taking out of the plugs, how the rods are used for removing the dirt, replacing the plugs, filling up the boiler, cleaning or burning out of the blast pipe, and the sweeping of the tubes, &c.

WHEN FILLING THE BOILER it will be seen that the regulator is left open as an outlet for the air which is displaced by the water in the boiler. It will also be noticed that the water does not show more than 2in. in the glass when cold. After the fires are lit, however, the water will be seen to expand considerably.

The cleaner, in the course of his work, has a splendid opportunity for inspection and should call the attention of his foreman to any defect in the motion, and always be on the look-out for missing nuts, split pins, or broken springs, &c.

Should the fitters be working on the engine much useful information can be obtained, if eyes and ears are kept open.

Fitters' Labourers

The writers are of opinion that it would be to the advantage of both companies and men if every cleaner could act as labourer to the fitters, if only for a short time. To the departmental heads, this course may at the first glance appear somewhat costly, as regards the changing of fitters' labourers just at the time when they are becoming useful. On the other hand, against the cost of learning should be placed the benefits accruing to the companies, through these very men in after life, when firing or driving, having greater confidence on account of this their fuller knowledge, when they are confronted with cases of engine failure, &c.

THE CLEANER, for his own protection, will do well to study carefully any shed regulations that may be posted by the company. The foreman should also ascertain by judicious questions from time to time that the cleaners have thoroughly understood the purport of these important instructions.

THE FOLLOWING SHED REGULATIONS are used by many railway companies:–

(1) When it is necessary to place engines in the shed they must first be brought to a stand outside, and must not be taken within the shed until the driver, or other authorised person in charge of the operations, has warned any men who may be working on or near the road on which the engine will travel, and when all is clear the engine must be brought in very slowly, an alarm whistle being given while this is being done.

(2) Before an engine is left, the cylinder cocks must be open; it

must have the hand brakes hard on, the regulator shut, and the reversing lever put out of gear.

(3) No engineman, engine turner, fireman, or other authorised person must move an engine, WHETHER IN STEAM OR NOT, without first personally satisfying himself that no cleaners or others are engaged in any work about the engine, or upon any engine or engines coupled to it, or standing within twenty yards of it, on the same line of rails. Any men so engaged must individually be clearly told that the engine is about to be moved, and the person giving the warning must obtain from each man as acknowledgement that he has heard and understood the warning, and such person must intimate to all concerned, when the movement of the engine is completed.

(4) When any men are employed cleaning, or working on an engine in the shed, a board with the words "Not to be moved" must be hung on the lamp iron at both ends of the engine, and the man in charge of the work which is being done must be responsible for seeing that this board is in position, and is removed when the cleaners or workmen have completed their duties.

(5) If any repairs are being executed, during which it is not advisable to move the engine, in addition to the "Not to Move" boards, two boards must be fixed with the words "Not to be Moved" – "Engine Disabled" one on the regulator and another in a prominent position on the buffer plank, and on no account must these boards be removed until the work is completed, and the fitter, boilermaker, or other person responsible for the work must see that they are exhibited before commencing operations, and must also be responsible for their removal when the work is completed.

(6) When it is necessary for any men to work on an engine, either in the way of cleaning, washing-out, or repairs, men thus employed must see that the hand brake is hard on, and that the regulator is secured by means of the locking bolt, and in cases where a locking bolt is not fitted, a clip must be used for securing the regulator handle. In the case of cleaners, the senior cleaner engaged on the engine will be responsible for seeing this is done.

(7) The only persons beside drivers and firemen allowed to move an engine in steam are the shed foreman, shed shunter, or men specially authorised. Firemen are not allowed to move engines except

when instructed by their drivers and when the driver is with them.

(8) Cleaners are not allowed to move engines in steam under any circumstances, and will render themselves liable to be instantly dismissed should they do so. When it is necessary for an engine to be moved for cleaning purposes, they must request the foreman or shed shunter to have it moved.

(9) When it is necessary to move an engine with the pinch bar or otherwise, the hand brake must be put on again as soon as the removal is completed.

(10) When men are working upon an engine which requires to be moved in the shed, or even reversed, they must be warned by the person doing this, and they must cease working while the engine is being moved or reversed.

(11) Men are forbidden from joining engines, or getting off engines, when in motion, or from riding on the footsteps or side plating of engine when in motion.

(12) Workmen, cleaners, and others are instructed to take every care to avoid accidents to themselves and their mates. No one is allowed to pass between the buffers of engines when they are at all near, but must go underneath.

(13) No engine must be worked in the shed yards without two men being on the foot-plate.

(14) Before any fire is put into a fire-box the gauge cocks must be tested, to ascertain that there is water in the boiler, and any person having occasion to empty a boiler will be held responsible for placing a board on the front of the firebox indicating that the boiler is empty.

(15) In cases where engines are left in the shed with the tenders or tanks empty, a board must be placed indicating that this is the case, or the words "Tank Empty," written plainly in a conspicuous place on the tender, viz., on the black paint near the brake handle.

By the time that the cleaner has thoroughly mastered the various details appertaining to his duties he will have commenced to learn the distinctive features of various types of engines, such as inside and outside cylinder engines for instance.

Inside cylinder engines have the cylinders fixed inside the framing, immediately underneath the smoke-box. Outside cylinder engines, as the name denotes, have the cylinders fixed outside the framing plates, and are coupled with rods direct to the driving wheels. Saddle tank engines are mostly used for pilot work, and have the tank containing the feed water fixed saddle wise on the top of the boiler. Tender engines are those with tenders attached, and are mostly used for quick traffic or long journeys. Tank engines carry their water in tanks on the sides of the boiler, and the coal in bunkers on their own framing, being mostly used for ordinary stopping trains or short journeys.

An engine with the driving and leading wheels coupled is known as "a four wheeled front coupled." When the driving and trailing wheels are coupled the engine is known as "a four wheeled back coupled."

THE DIAGRAMS OF WHEEL ARRANGEMENTS are intended to be of assistance to the rising cleaner; in acquiring a knowledge of the distinguishing features appertaining to the different types of coupled and non-coupled engines.

The first diagram is a 2–2–2 tender passenger engine, without side rods, and would be known as a single wheeled engine. This type was designed for high speeds, with moderate train loads, and has therefore been chiefly used in the past for express passenger work. The second example also shows a 4–2–2 uncoupled, tender, passenger engine, with the front end supported upon a bogie, and the trailing end by carrying wheels, and would be described as a single wheeled bogie engine, with trailing carrying boxes. This type has been much used in the past for express passenger work, but is now being gradually displaced by coupled engines of greater tractive power, although it may be mentioned that many record runs stand to the credit of these single wheeled passenger engines.

The third diagram illustrates a simple form of 2–4–2 coupled engine suitable for either goods or passenger traffic, and the wheel arrangement is also adaptable for either tank or tender engines. This type would be classed as a four-wheeled coupled, with leading and trailing carrying boxes, and is mostly used for tank engines, since the wheel base provides equal flexibility whether the engine be running in a forward or backward direction. The 4–4–0 type illustrated in the fourth diagram is known as a four-wheeled coupled, with leading bogie, and is extensively used in this country for both express passenger and fast goods trains.

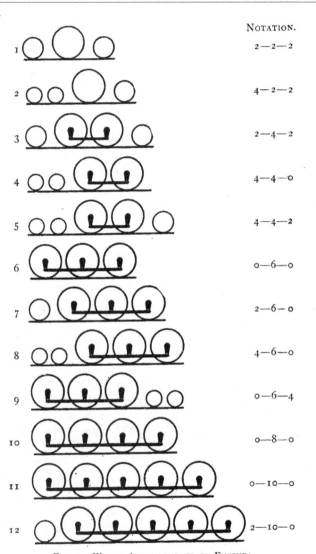

FIG. 1.—WHEEL ARRANGEMENTS OF ENGINES.

The fifth diagram illustrates the well-known "Atlantic" type of 4–4–2 tender passenger engine, and is a four-wheeled coupled, with trailing carrying boxes. This type is mostly used in conjunction with outside cylinders, and was first put into British railroad practice about the year 1898. Since their introduction, these engines have been extensively adopted by the principal railway companies for working heavy passenger traffic.

The sixth example is a six-wheeled coupled, and may almost be claimed as the standard goods engine in British railroad engineering practice. Owing to the superior adhesive qualities of this combination of coupled wheels, this type of 0–6–0 engine may be fitted with a tender and used for working heavy or fast goods trains, or be designed as a tank engine, in which case it would be suitable for either shunting purposes or local goods traffic.

The seventh diagram is a 2–6–0 type of tender engine, suitable for heavy or fast goods traffic, and would be known as a six-wheeled coupled with leading carrying boxes.

The eighth type is a 4–6–0 tender engine, suitable for the modern heavy fast passenger service, and would be described as a six-wheeled coupled with leading bogie. This is a powerful type in which haulage capacity and speed qualities are combined, thereby rendering these engines also available for heavy fast or perishable goods traffic.

The 0–6–4 arrangement of wheels, illustrated in the ninth diagram, is a six-wheeled coupled, with trailing bogie, suitable for tank engines, and may be used for either goods or passenger traffic. The three last diagrams are types of wheel arrangements, as adopted for the modern and very powerful goods engines. These types would be known respectively as 0–8–0 or eight-wheeled coupled; 0–10–0, or ten-wheeled coupled; and 2–10–0, or ten-wheeled coupled with leading carrying boxes.

FOLLOWING THE TYPES OF ENGINES, the cleaner is recommended to learn the method of classifying trains by their head lamps. The following is the code of head lamps used by most railway companies:–

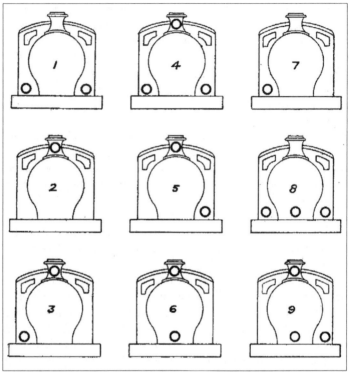

FIG. 2. –ARRANGEMENT OF HEAD LAMPS.

1. Express passenger train or Break-down train going to clear the line.
2. Ordinary passenger train or Break-down train not going to clear the line.
3. Fish, meat, fruit, horse, cattle, or perishables train composed of coaching stock.
4. Empty coaching stock train.
5. Fish, meat, or fruit train, composed of goods, stock, express cattle, or Express goods train, Class A.
6. Express cattle or Express goods train, Class B.
7. Light engine, or light engines coupled together, or engine and break.
8. Through goods, Mineral, or ballast train.
9. Ordinary goods or Mineral train, stopping at intermediate stations.

THE TENDER

THE TENDER, Fig. 60 on page 62, is erected upon its own framing, and is therefore a separate vehicle attached to the engine by means of the draw bar D. It is designed with a water tank W for the boiler feed supply, and bunkers B to carry the required amount of coal, proper receptacles being also provided for the necessary tools and lamps, etc. The draw bar, which couples the engine to the tender, is made in the form of a long eye bolt, the end containing the eye being connected to the engine by means of a strong pin 3ins. diam. The straight end of the bar is usually about 4ins. diam., and passes through the tender drag box Y, being secured by a 4in. nut well tightened home, and secured in position by a split cotter.

THE FRAMING is made from mild steel plates about ⅞ in. thick, which are straightened, slotted and drilled as described for the engine frame plates. Cast steel hornplates, usually in the form of single angle plates, are riveted to the horns with ⅞ in. diam. cold steel rivets, care being taken that they are fixed parallel, in order that the axle boxes, which are afterwards fitted, may work smoothly without any sign of jar or knock.

THE SPRING BRACKETS, which eventually support the whole weight of the tender when attached to the bearing springs, are also riveted to the main frame plates. Angle irons about 6in. by 3in. by ¾ in. section are riveted to the top edge of the framing and extend the full length of the tender so as to form a base for the water tank. The frame plates placed on edge are then set square and parallel to each other to the required gauge, being held in position at the front end by the box front plate, which is securely fastened to the frames by angle irons riveted to the framing ends.

THE BACK OR TRAILING BUFFER PLATE is secured in a similar manner, the draw bar, which passes through the centre of the plate, being- held by suitable springs or strong rubber pads R about 6in. in thickness. The middle parts of the frame plates are stayed by strong tee irons, which are fitted from side to side midway between each of the leading, middle and trailing wheels. An inside framing made from iron or mild steel plates about 12in. by ½ in. is fitted the full length of the tender about 9in. or 10 in. from the outer fram¬ing. The inside frame plates are secured to the outer plates by box brackets and are finished at the top with angle irons which give additional support to the tank bottom. The back plate, which forms the drag box, is fixed about 3ft. or 3ft. 6in. behind the front drag box plate, and is secured by angle irons tc the outside framing. The automatic, or the steam brake cylinder A, whichever is adopted, is attached to the underside of this plate, and the brake-shaft, which passes transversely across the framing, is held by brackets secured to the outer frames by ¾ in. diam. cold steel rivets.

THE DIAMETER OF THE WHEELS varies from 3 to 4 ft. in the different designs of tender. They are usually made with cast steel centres and rolled steel tyres, the process of manufacture being invariably as described for the engine wheels. The axle boxes, generally in the form of an iron or steel casting, are so designed that the brass bearing fitted therein may be withdrawn for repairs or renewal, when relieved of the weight of the tender. The axle journals are about 6in. diam. by 10in. long, and are lubricated in different ways, as by ordinary worsted trimmings, or from an oil well contained in the bottom of the axle boxes. The latter method is perhaps the most efficient, a pad of cotton waste or some such material being packed inside the oil wells, thus retaining the oil, which is thereby continually lubricating the journals. Special arrangements, such as leather or metal rings, are fitted to prevent the escape of oil from the back of the boxes, and for keeping out dirt or grit when the engine is running.

THE BEARING SPRINGS are of the laminated type, consisting of about 10 to 14 plates, which are held together by a buckle. Side flange friction is reduced as much as possible by fitting a loose sliding- shoe on top of the middle axle boxes, and also by giving' the boxes a small amount of side play.

THE TANK BOTTOM, which also forms the tender foot plate, is made from mild steel plate ⅜ in. thick, and is secured to the framing and to the angle irons, which are fixed the full length of the tender. The tank sides, which are made from ¼in. or ⁵⁄₁₆in. plate, have a large flat area, and are therefore suitably strengthened with internal gusset or plate stays to withstand the heavy rush of water that takes place when running over rough portions of the road.

FROM 4 TO 5 TONS is about the average amount of coal necessary for an ordinary journey, and this is carried in a suitable bunker formed with an inclined bottom, so that the vibration of the tender will assist in bringing the coal forward within easy reach of the fireman. A cornice or coal guard is also fitted along the top of the sides and back of the tender to prevent the coal falling on to the road.

A tool box with sliding doors is often formed on the front of the tank immediately over the coal bunker, and is fitted with locking arrangements enabling the tools to be left secure when the enginemen come off duty. When not provided in this manner separate tool boxes are placed in convenient positions on the top of the tank.

FOR FILLING THE TANK with water an aperture fitted with a lid is formed in the top of the tank about 4ft. from the trail¬ing end. To meet the boiler feed requirements of the large engines now in use a tank capacity of 4,000 gallons or 40,000 lbs. is often necessary, and as a consequence the dead load attached to the engine is considerably increased by this large body of water. Seeing that 4 tons of average coal will approximately evaporate over 30 tons of water, it is obvious that a reduction in the weight of water carried is of the greatest importance.

By the adoption of the water pick-up apparatus, the dead load may be greatly lessened by reducing the size of the tank, and long runs may be made without the loss of time that occurs when having to stop at a column for water. The apparatus consists of a hinged scoop S, which may be lowered by the enginemen when passing over the water trough. These troughs are usually about 17ins. or 18ins. wide by 6ins. deep and are fixed between the rails. A pipe casting C in the form of a bend is fixed to face the leading end of the engine, and secured by a flange about 15ins. diam. to the underside of the tank bottom. The scoop is fitted with a hinged joint H to the lower end of this pipe, and is connected by rods P to a screw T actuated by the hand wheel E which is fitted upon the front of the tank for

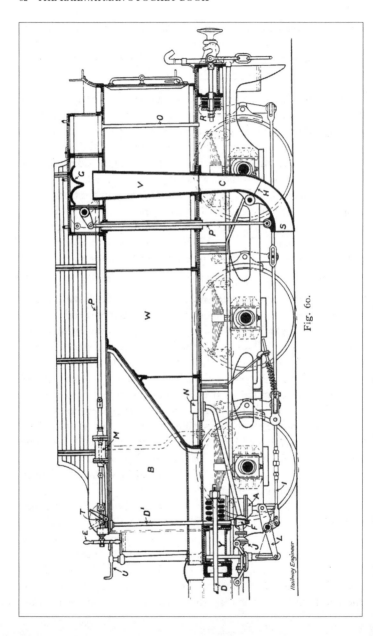

Fig. 60.

Railway Engineer

lowering, and to a steam cylinder M or other device to give assistance when raising the scoop from the water. A vertical pipe V is fixed inside the tank having a flange similar to the pipe below, and is secured by eight ¾in. bolts which pass through both flanges and the tank bottom. The internal pipe is made in different forms and may be curved at the top to throw the water downward, or be a plain vertical pipe tapering to a larger diameter at the top than the bottom with the discharge end about 7ins. above the water level when the tank is full. In the latter case a guard G is fixed above the pipe to check the velocity of the water, which thus falls back into the tank, an overflow 0 being also provided to prevent the tender top becoming flooded. The scoop is about 10 ins, wide, and dips from 1½ to 2 ½ ins. into the water when in its lowest position, sufficient clearance being thus provided between the scoop and trough bottom to allow for wear of tyres and springs, etc. The normal water level in the trough is automatically maintained by suitable valves or pumps, and the length of the trough is determined by the amount of water required, or the available water supply, etc., 500 yards being about the average, although troughs up to 700 yds. in length are in use. The troughs are fixed at a level and straight length of the line, and are located as far as circumstances will permit to supply the most suitable water for boiler feed purposes at economical rates.

THE SPEED OF THE TRAIN imparts the force necessary for lifting the water into the tank, and it will be found that from 15 to 20 miles must be attained before the water can be raised to the required height. At a speed of from 22 to 25 miles per hour, with a dip of 2ins., considerably over 2,000 gallons may be lifted into the tank when passing over a trough of average length, the quantity of water raised, however, remaining practically the same for any higher speed. Considerable resistance is exerted against the scoop as it moves through the inert body of water, and for this reason addi¬tional power is required to raise it, hence the necessity for steam or vacuum cylinders, etc., to assist when lifting the scoop into its normal running position. Draw bar-pull diagrams show that the resistance of the water under certain conditions may be sufficient to absorb all the pulling power of the engine while it passes over the troughs with the scoop down.

The importance of accurately knowing the amount of water in the tender tank for boiler feed purposes has already been mentioned, and any method whereby this may be automatically or continuously ascertainable will therefore be of interest.

The Areo water level indicator, fig. 61, as supplied by Messrs. Sydney Stone and Co., is so simple in design and construction that the risks of failure, due to the vibratory movements of the engine or tender, are reduced to a minimum. The apparatus consists of a small air chamber or generator (a) which is fixed at the bottom of the tender tank, and connected from the top by a small air tube (c) to a graduated gauge (d), which is placed on the boiler front plate in full view of the driver.

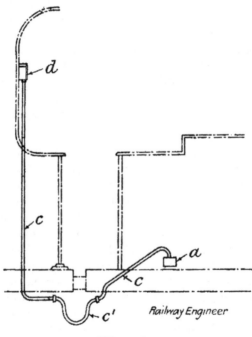

Fig. 61.

The air pipes (c) (c) on the engine and tender are connected by the flexible pipe (c¹) as shown, and transmit any pressure due to head of water above (a) to the dial (d), which is graduated according to the depth of the tank.

It is claimed that the apparatus is unaffected by frost and cannot fluctuate, since air is the only medium employed for transmitting the pressure from the water in the tank to the graduated gauge.

The feed valves F, fig. 60, are placed on the extreme ends of the tank and are actuated by handles D^1 for regulating the supply, brass dome shaped sieves N being fixed inside the tank over the outlet to the valves to prevent the injectors being damaged or choked by solid substances which may have entered with the feed supply.

To allow for the difference of movement between engine and tender flexible feed pipe connections are made, the necessary flexibility being obtained by fitting the pipes with ball and socket joints J as well as a sliding gland to give the required end movement.

CAST-IRON SAND-BOXES are placed in convenient positions upon the footplate for use when running tender first or to be used in conjunction with the engine sanding gear, when the rails are exceptionally bad, iron pipes being fitted to conduct the sand from the boxes to the rails. The sand valves are usually of the butterfly type, worked by handles which may be regulated to supply the proper quantity, special care being also taken by protecting the boxes to prevent the sand from becoming damped by any leakage of water.

TENDERS are fitted with a hand brake for use in addition to the automatic vacuum, Westinghouse, or steam brake when entering a terminus or when stopping at signals, etc. The brake handle U is conveniently placed in front of the tank, being secured thereto by suitable brackets, the shaft passing through the footplate to the brake lever L, which is actuated by a screw and nut below. This lever is connected to the brake shaft, and the necessary brake power is transmitted by pull rods I to the brake cross shaft and thence to the brake blocks.

LNER

RESOLUTION OF
BOARD OF DIRECTORS.

At a meeting of the Board of Directors of the London and North Eastern Railway Company, held at Marylebone, on the 24th day of June, 1932, minute 1486.

IT WAS RESOLVED—

"That the following Rules be and are hereby approved and adopted for observance by the employees of the London and North Eastern Railway Company, from the 1st January, 1933, and that all former Rules which are inconsistent therewith or are made obsolete thereby be and are hereby cancelled."

JAMES McLAREN
Secretary.

Alterations of, and additions to, the Rules approved and adopted by the Board of Directors on the 24th June, 1932 (Minute No. 1486) have been approved and adopted by the Board at subsequent meetings. Such alterations and additions were shown in Supplements Nos. 1 to 14 inclusive and are incorporated in the following Rules.

THESE RULES *have been agreed to generally by the Companies parties to the Railway Clearing System, and apply—except where a note to the contrary is shown and subject to modifications which may be made from time to time, due notice of which will be given—to the London and North Eastern Railway Company's undertaking, whether in respect of their own engines, trains, and employees, or those of other Companies running over their line. The employees of the London and North Eastern Railway Company working over the lines of other Companies will be bound by these Rules, and such modifications thereof as may be issued from time to time, and where the Company owning the line have any exceptional or additional Rules and Regulations, they will also be bound by the exceptional or additional Rules and Regulations of that Company.*

Each employee supplied with this book must make himself acquainted with, and will be held responsible for the observance of, the following Rules.

CONTROL AND WORKING OF STATIONS.

1. Station Masters are responsible for—

(i.) the security and protection of the buildings and property at the station.

(ii.) the efficient discharge of duties devolving upon all employees engaged at the station or within its limits, and for promptly reporting any neglect of duty on the part of such employees.

(iii.) the general working of the station being carried out in strict accordance with the Company's regulations, and, as far as practicable, for giving personal attention to the shunting of trains and all other operations affecting the safety of the railway.

(iv.) the employees under them connected with the operative working of the railway being in possession of a copy of these Rules, and for the proper, distribution of the working time-tables,

appendices, and other notices having reference to the working of the railway.

(v.) making themselves thoroughly acquainted with the duties of the Signalmen under their control and for frequently visiting the signal boxes to maintain proper supervision over the working.

(vi.) a daily inspection of the station, also the cleanliness and neatness of all premises (including closets and urinals), signboards, &c.

(vii.) all orders and instructions being duly recorded and complied with, and books and returns being regularly written up.

(viii.) the proper exhibition at the station and offices of the Company's Bye-laws, Carriers' Act, list of fares, statutory and other notices.

(ix.) promptly reporting complaints made by the public.

(x.) stores being properly and economically used.

(xi.) exhibiting in their offices up-to-date lists of the names and addresses of employees (including Fogsignalmen) connected with the traffic working.

2. All employees attached to a station, or employed in an area which is under the control of the Station Master, are subject to the Station Master's authority and direction in the working of the railway.

3.   Every exertion must be made for the expeditious despatch of the station duties, and for ensuring the punctuality of the trains.

4. (a.) The cleaning, trimming and lighting of all lamps must be carefully and regularly performed.

Oil lamps must be taken to the appointed places to be cleaned and trimmed.

(b.) Signal spectacles, lenses, reflectors and glasses must be kept thoroughly clean.

5. (a)Luggage and parcels must not, where the width of the platform will admit, be left within six feet of the edge of the platform; platform trollies, barrows, &c., not in use must be kept back close to the buildings or to the wall or fence at the back of the platform, with their handles so placed as to avoid the risk of persons stumbling over them. When necessary, platform trollies, barrows, &c., must be so secured as to prevent them from moving.

(b) Unauthorised persons must not be allowed to use trollies, barrows, &c.

6. Platforms, crossing places, steps, ramps and approaches to stations must, when necessary, be strewn with sand, small ballast, or ashes, or be otherwise treated to avoid accidents by slipping. Such places must also be kept free from snow.

The permanent-way staff must assist as far as possible. Small ballast or sand will be supplied on application to the Permanent-way Inspector for the district.

7. (a) Each passenger train after completing its journey, and all vehicles detached from such trains at stations as "empty," must be searched.

(b) When a compartment becomes vacant the windows must be closed when this can be done without causing delay to the train. They must also be kept closed and the ventilators open when the carriages are not in use. The windows of Guards' compartments and vans in which a Guard is not riding must also be kept closed.

8. When a passenger train is entering a station at which it is booked to stop, as well as after it has come to a stand, employees must call out clearly the name of the station and of stations at which the train stops during the journey.

At junction stations employees must also announce the changes for connecting trains.

9.(a)   The doors of vehicles must be fastened before the train leaves the station, and no door must be opened to allow a passenger to alight from or enter a train before it has come to a stand, or after it has started.

(b) Passengers showing signs of their intention to alight from, or join, a train in motion, must be warned against doing so.

10. Without special authority a passenger train must not be stopped where it is not booked to call, to take up or set down passengers.

11. In the case of a passenger train booked to call only when required to take up passengers, the necessary fixed signals must, when the stop has to be made, be exhibited against it; and a competent man appointed by the Station Master must exhibit a red hand signal from the station platform, to intimate to the Driver that his train is required to stop; such red hand signal need not, however, be exhibited where a fixed signal is in such a position that a train stopped at it is at the platform.

12. (a) Where specified trains have to be examined by Carriage and Wagon Examiners, the Station Master, before giving the signal to start such trains, must satisfy himself that the work has been completed, and that the vehicles are in order.

(b) Where Examiners are not available, steps must be taken by the Station Master to have any defect remedied, and if this cannot be done the defective vehicle must, if necessary, be detached from the train.

(c) At stations where brake-testing and gas-charging are performed, the Station Master must satisfy himself that the duties have been completed.

13. (a) When a crane is in use and the jib, or any other portion of it, obstructs or fouls any line in use for traffic purposes, or whenever, during the loading or unloading of timber, iron or other articles, any running line is liable to be fouled, the person in charge of the work must obtain the sanction of both the Station Master and Signalman and satisfy himself that the proper signals are exhibited until the operation is completed.

If the crane has to be used at a siding not protected by fixed signals, a Handsignalman must, when necessary, be provided to protect the operation in accordance with Rule 217.

(b) Except where specially authorised, timber or other articles must not be loaded or unloaded after dusk, or during fog or falling snow, if any running line is liable to be fouled by the operation.

(c) Cranes must be kept locked or otherwise secured when not in use.

(d) Timber Loaders and other persons working at a station or siding will be under the control of the Station Master, who, whilst they are so employed, must exercise the same supervision over them as over his own staff.

14. When a horse is used on the railway a man must, on the approach and during the passing of any train, hold its head, whether the horse be drawing vehicles or not.

15. (a) A privately-owned engine under its own power must not be allowed upon any running line, unless authorised by the General Manager or Operating Superintendent.

(b) Before any privately-owned engine, or contractor's wagon, is accepted for conveyance on its own wheels, it must be examined by the Locomotive or Wagon Department, as the case may be, and special arrangements made as to the train by which it is to travel. Guards and others concerned must satisfy themselves that this has been done before allowing the engine or wagon to travel.

16. At terminal stations, and other places where there are dead-end bays, after sunset and during fog or falling snow, and otherwise where special instructions exist, a red light must be placed on the buffer-stops of arrival lines or on any train or vehicles left on such lines so as to be plainly visible to the Driver of an incoming train.

17. (a) Clocks at stations and signal boxes must be corrected as may be necessary on receipt of the daily time signal, which is sent in accordance with the special instructions on the subject. Any defects must at once be reported.

(b) At stations where the time signal is not received the Station Master must obtain the precise time from the Guard of the first stopping train commencing its journey after 10.0 a.m. and correct the station clocks as may be necessary.

(c) When on duty each Guard must satisfy himself that his watch is correct.

FIXED SIGNALS.

18. Fixed signals consist of distant, stop, and subsidiary signals.

In certain instances signals are repeated, in which cases the additional signals are known as repeating signals.

Automatic signals are signals controlled by the passage of trains.

Semi-automatic signals are signals which are controlled by the passage of trains and in addition can be controlled from a signal box or ground frame.

19. (a)Semaphore signals are generally of the two-position type, the indications being shown thus:—

BY DAY.   **BY NIGHT.**

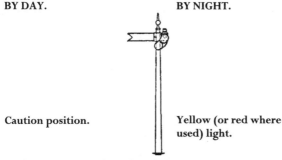

Caution position.   Yellow (or red where
                                     used) light.

(b) Other types of signals include:–

(i.) Three-position semaphore signals–the indications being shown thus:–

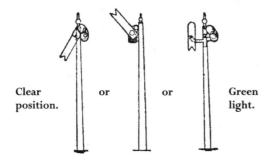

Clear   or   or   Green
position.   light.

DISTANT SIGNALS

(ii.) Colour light signals–not provided with semaphore arms, the day and night indications being given by means of lights only, i.e., red for Danger, yellow for Caution, and green for Clear.

London Midland and Scottish Company's addition:–

In some cases colour light signals will exhibit two yellow lights. This indication means–Pass next signal at restricted speed, and if applicable to a junction may denote that the points are set for a diverging route over which the speed restriction shown in the Appendix [not included here] applies.

BY DAY.　　　　　　　　　　　　　　　　**BY NIGHT.**

Danger
position
　　　　　　　　　　　　　　　　　　　　　Red
　　　　　　　　　　　　　　　　　　　　　Light

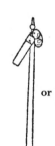
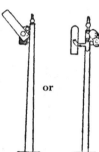

Clear
position.　　　or　　　or
　　　　　　　　　　　　　　　　　　　　　Green
　　　　　　　　　　　　　　　　　　　　　light.

BY DAY.

Danger　　　　　Caution　　　Clear
position　　　　　position　　　position

(iii.) Repeating signals of the banner type consisting of a black arm in a circular frame, illuminated at night.

(iv.) Subsidiary signals in the form of disc signals, or of the banner type with red or yellow arm in a circular frame, or position light signals, or semaphore signals with small arms—the normal indications being—

By day.	By night.
Red disc.	Red light or white light.
Yellow disc.	Yellow light.
Red arm in horizontal position in a circular frame or on a white disc.	Red light, white light or the day normal indication being illuminated.
Yellow arm in horizontal position in a circular frame or on a white disc.	Yellow light or the day normal indication being illuminated.
Position light signals with two white lights, or one red or yellow light on the left and one white light on the right, in horizontal position, or no lights.	Same as by day.
Small red semaphore arm, or small white semaphore arm with red stripes, in the horizontal position.	Red light, white light, or no light.
Small yellow semaphore arm in the horizontal position.	Yellow light.

The Proceed indication by day is given by the disc being turned off or the arm lowered or raised or in the case of position light signals by two white lights at an angel of 45 degrees; and by night by a green light or the day Proceed indication being illuminated or in the case of position light signals by two white lights at an angle of 45 degrees.

In some cases the signals are distinguished thus:—
Calling-on—   by the letter C.
Warning—   "   "   W.
Shunt-ahead—   "   "   S.

Ground signals (colour light)—the normal indication being a yellow or red light and the Proceed indication a green light.

(c) Automatic stop signals are identified by a white plate with a horizontal black band.

Semi-automatic stop signals are identified by a white plate bearing the word "SEMI" above a horizontal black band.

(d) Back lights, where provided for fixed signals, show a white light to the Signalman when the signals are at Danger, and are obscured when the signals are in the Clear position. In the case of position light signals where back lights are provided, they are also exhibited in some cases when the signals are at Clear.

(e) Fixed signals, as a rule, are so placed as to indicate by their positions the lines to which they apply. Where more than one stop or subsidiary signal is fixed on the same side of a post the top signal applies to the line on the extreme left, and the second signal to the line next in order from the left and so on.

At some diverging points, only one semaphore arm or colour light signal is provided together with an indicator exhibiting a letter or number showing the line over which the train will run,

or

only one colour light signal is provided together with a junction indicator exhibiting a line of white light or lights by day and by night when a Proceed aspect is given for a diverging route (see diagram below); for movements along the straight route no junction indication will be exhibited.

Indication 1 is the equivalent of signal 1 when "Off."

Indication 2 is the equivalent of signal 2 when "Off."

Indication 3 is the equivalent of signal 3 when "Off."

Indications 4, 5 and 6 relate to routes on the right hand of the straight line and apply in a similar manner.

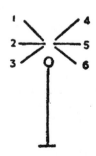

(f) Except in the case of automatic signals or where otherwise authorised, the normal position of fixed signals is Danger, or Caution in the case of distant signals.

NOTE.—*Additions to this Rule are contained in separate publications issued by the Companies concerned.*

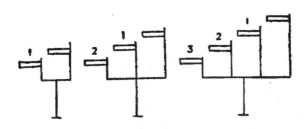

DISTANT SIGNALS.

20. (a) Distant signals are placed at some distance in rear of the home signals to which they apply, and where necessary below the home, starting or advanced starting signal, applicable to the same line, of the signal box in rear.

(b) Where only one distant signal is provided for a diverging junction such signal applies to all trains approaching it.

(c) The Caution position of a distant signal indicates to a Driver that he must be prepared to stop at the home signal to which it applies.

STOP SIGNALS (Home, Starting and Advanced Starting).

21. (a) Where starting signals are provided the home signal must not be passed at Danger except as follow:—

Exceptions.

(i.) *When subsidiary signals are lowered (Rules 45 and 47).*

(ii.) *When a train is required to enter an obstructed line for the purpose of rendering assistance and the Driver is so authorised by the Signalman.*

(iii.) *When signal is defective or cannot be lowered owing to failure of apparatus or during repairs (Rules 77, 78 and 81).*

(iv.) *When single line working is in operation during repairs or obstruction (Rule 197).*

London Midland and Scottish Company's additional Exception:—

(v.) When necessary for an engine to be brought to the rear of a train to attach or detach vehicles, or to remove vehicles from the line. (Rule 116 (b).)

Where a home signal controls the entrance of trains into the section ahead the provisions of Rule 38 apply to such signal.

(b) Where a starting signal is not provided and it is necessary for a train which has been stopped at the home signal to be brought within that signal before the line ahead is clear, the Signalman before lowering the home signal must verbally inform the Driver as to the state of the line ahead and what is required of him.

If, when the train is stopped at the home signal, it is not possible for the verbal communication to be made Rule 40 must be observed.

When the line ahead is clear, the signal for the train to proceed must be given by the Signalman showing the Driver a green hand signal held steadily.

22. (a) Where advanced starting signals are provided, the starting signal must not be passed at Danger except as follow:—

Exceptions.

(i.) *When subsidiary signals are lowered (Rules 45 and 47).*

(ii.) *When a train is required to enter an obstructed line for the purpose of rendering assistance and the Driver is so authorised by the Signalman.*

(iii.) *When signal is defective, or cannot be lowered owing to failure of apparatus or during repairs (Rules 77, 78 and 81).*

(iv.) *When single line working is in operation during repairs or obstruction (Rule 197).*

(b) Home signals where starting signals are not provided, starting signals where advanced starting signals are not provided, and advanced starting signals, control the entrance of trains into the section ahead, and must not be passed at Danger except as follow:—

Exceptions.

(i.) *When calling-on, warning or shunt-ahead signals are lowered (Rules 44, 45 and 46).*

(ii.) *Where the position of siding connections or crossover roads renders it necessary for the signal controlling the entrance to the section ahead to be passed for shunting purposes and a shunt-ahead signal is not provided, a Driver may, for this purpose, pass the signal at Danger upon being directed to do so by the Signalman, either verbally or by a green hand signal held steadily, but he must not go forward on his journey until the signal controlling the entrance to the section ahead has been lowered.*

(iii.) *During failure of instruments or bells when it is necessary for a train to be brought within the protection of the home signal, in accordance with Block Regulation 25, clause (e), and a shunt-ahead signal is not provided, upon the Driver being instructed verbally by the Signalman, but the Driver must not proceed on his journey until the starting (or advanced starting) signal has been lowered, or until authorised to do so in accordance with clause (b) of Rule 37.*

(iv.) *[Deleted.]*

(v.) *When signal is defective, or cannot be lowered owing to failure of apparatus or during repairs. (Rules 77, 78 and 81).*

(vi.) *When single line working is in operation during repairs or obstruction. (Rule 197.)*

(vii.) *When a train is required to enter an obstructed section and the Driver is instructed verbally by the Signalman. (Block Regulation 14.)*

(viii.) *When an engine (or train) is required to enter a section to examine the line, and the Driver is instructed verbally by the Signalman.(**Block Regulation 14A**.)*

(ix.) *When necessary to allow the front portion of a divided train to proceed into the section ahead. (Rule 182.)* (This exception does not apply on the Great Western Railway.)

(x.) *When necessary for a train to follow first portion of a divided train. (Block Regulation 20.)*

(xi.) *When necessary for a train to travel through section after runaway train or vehicles are removed from the section. (Block Regulations 22 and 23.)*

London Midland and Scottish Company's additional Exception:–

(xii.) When necessary at stations where absolute block working is in force for an engine to be brought to the rear of a train to attach or detach vehicles or to remove vehicles from the section. (Rule 116 (b).)

23.(a) When a stop signal is at Danger the stop signal next in rear of it worked from the same signal box must not be lowered for an approaching train until the train is close to such signal and has been brought quite, or nearly, to a stand.

During fog or falling snow, the Driver of a train stopped, or nearly stopped, at a signal next in rear of a starting signal must, when practicable, be verbally informed that he is only to draw forward towards the starting signal.

NOTE.—*This clause (a) does not apply to multiple-aspect signals.*

(b) During fog or falling snow—unless track circuit or other apparatus is provided in connection with the advanced starting signal to avoid the necessity for trainmen having to go to the signal box to carry out Rule 55—a train must not be drawn past the starting signal towards the advanced starting signal except for station duties or shunting purposes, or where special instructions are issued to the contrary.

(c) The Driver of any train which has been stopped or brought nearly to a stand in accordance with clause (a), must, after the signal has been lowered, draw slowly forward to the next signal and be prepared to stop at the signal box if necessary. When proceeding towards a starting or advanced starting signal at Danger, he must (except for station duties or shunting purposes, or as shown below) only proceed as far as is necessary to leave the last vehicle well clear of junction points and junction crossings, and, as far as practicable, within sight of the Signalman. Where there are no junction points or junction crossings the Driver must bring his train to a stand in a convenient position for the carrying out of Rule 55.

Where track circuit or other apparatus is provided in connection with the starting or advanced starting signal, to avoid the necessity for trainmen having to go to the signal box to carry out Rule 55, the Driver must draw forward to the starting or advanced starting signal.

Southern Company's amendment to clause (c):—

A Driver must in all cases draw forward to the starting signal or advanced starting signal, as the case may be.

24. When a Signalman wishes to communicate verbally with a Driver he must stop the train at the signal next in rear of the signal box for this purpose, but if it is not then possible for the verbal communication to be made, he must lower the signal (or subsidiary signal where provided) for the train to draw forward, and stop it at the signal box by exhibiting a red hand signal. The Driver must not proceed until he clearly understands the verbal communication and has received the necessary authority.

25.(a) When a train is allowed to go forward under Block Regulation 5 and a stop signal is provided in advance of the box, the Signalman must, if the train has not already passed the home signal, bring it quite or nearly to a stand at that signal before lowering it, and, unless a fixed warning signal or warning indication is provided, must as the train is approaching the box exhibit to the Driver a green hand signal, held steadily, which the Driver must acknowledge by giving a short whistle as an indication that he understands that the section is clear to the next home signal, but that the station or junction ahead is blocked. The necessary fixed signals may then be lowered for the train to proceed. If the Driver does not acknowledge the hand signal the signal controlling the entrance to the section ahead must not be lowered until the train has been brought to a stand at it.

If there is not a stop signal in advance of the box, the Signalman must, unless a fixed warning signal or warning indication is provided, stop the train in accordance with Rule 40, and verbally instruct the Driver that the section is clear to the next home signal but that the station or junction ahead is blocked, after which a green hand signal, held steadily, must be exhibited to the Driver.

If the train is assisted by an engine in rear, or two trains are coupled together, a green hand signal, held steadily, must be exhibited to the Driver of each engine.

Where a warning signal or warning indication is provided the green hand signal must not be exhibited.

(b) Except where instructions are issued to the contrary, when a train has passed the signal box and is brought to a stand owing to the signal controlling the entrance to the section ahead being at Danger, the lowering of such signal must be taken by the Driver as an indication that the section is clear to the next home signal but that the station or junction ahead is blocked, and he must regulate the speed of his train accordingly.

REPEATING SIGNALS.

26. Repeating signals, where provided, are placed in the rear of, and repeat the indication given by, the signals to which they apply.

When a repeating signal indicates that the stop signal is at Danger, the Driver must proceed cautiously towards the stop signal.

MULTIPLE-ASPECT SIGNALS.

27. Where three-aspect signals are provided, the Caution aspect indicates to a Driver that he must be prepared to stop at the next signal, and the Clear aspect indicates that he must be prepared to find the next signal showing either the Caution or Clear aspect.

Where colour light signals having more than three aspects are provided, one yellow light indicates to a Driver that he must be prepared to stop at the next signal, and two yellow lights indicate that he must be prepared to find the next signal showing one yellow light.

London and North Eastern Company's amendment to second paragraph:–

Where colour light signals having more than three aspects are provided, one yellow light indicates to a Driver that he must be prepared to stop at the next signal, and two yellow lights indicate that he must be prepared to pass the next signal at restricted speed.

London Midland and Scottish Company's amendment to second paragraph:–

Where colour light signals having more than three aspects are provided, one yellow light indicates to a Driver that he must be prepared to stop at the next signal, and two yellow lights indicate that he must be prepared to pass the next signal at restricted speed, and if applicable to a junction may denote that the points are set for a diverging route over which the speed restriction shown in the Appendix applies.

SUBSIDIARY SIGNALS.

Calling-on Signals.

28. (a) Calling-on signals, where provided, are placed below the signal controlling the entrance to the section ahead, and when lowered authorise the Driver to proceed forward cautiously into the section ahead as far as the line is clear.

The lowering of the calling-on signal does not authorise the next stop signal to be passed at Danger.

(b) Except where authorised, the calling-on signal must not be lowered until the train has been brought to a stand at it.

Warning Signals.

29. (a) Warning signals, where provided, are placed below stop signals, and when the warning signal is lowered the Driver must understand that the line is clear only as far as the next stop signal. The lowering of a warning signal fixed under the signal controlling the entrance to the section ahead must be taken as an indication that the section is clear to the next home signal but that the station or junction ahead is blocked, and the

Driver must regulate the speed of his train accordingly.

(b) The warning signal must not be lowered until the train has been brought quite, or nearly, to a stand at it.

Shunt-ahead Signals.

30. Shunt-ahead signals, where provided, are placed below the signal controlling the entrance to the section ahead, and, when lowered, authorise the latter signal to be passed at Danger for shunting purposes only, and a train must not proceed on its journey until the signal controlling the entrance to the section has been lowered.

Draw-ahead and Shunting Signals.

31. Draw-ahead signals, where provided, are placed below stop signals not controlling the entrance to the section ahead.

Shunting signals are used to regulate the passage of trains from a siding to a running line, from a running line to a siding, between one running line and another, and to control shunting operations.

Draw-ahead and shunting signals apply when lowered as far as the line is clear towards the next signal only, but the lowering or turning off of such signals does not authorise the next signal to be passed at Danger.

Except as provided for in Rules 40 and 96, the draw-ahead signal may be lowered after the train has been brought quite or nearly to a stand at it.

Shunting signals of the types described below may be passed, without being turned off or lowered, for movements in a direction for which the signal when turned off or lowered does not apply:—

Signal having a yellow arm or disc.

    "   "   " yellow arm on a white disc.

    "   "   " yellow light.

Position light signal having yellow and white lights.

SIGNAL CONTROLLING EXIT FROM SIDING.

32. (a) Where a signal is provided to control the exit from a siding and a train is ready to depart, a Driver must not proceed until such signal has been lowered, nor must a Driver, whilst waiting for the signal to be lowered, allow his engine to stand foul of any other line.

(b) When a signal applies to more than one siding and more than one engine is in the sidings, a Driver must not move towards the signal so as to foul any other siding until he has been instructed to do so by the person in charge of the shunting operations.

TRAINS SHUNTING OR RUNNING IN WRONG DIRECTION.

33.Distant, home, starting, advanced starting, and subsidiary signals placed under stop signals apply only to trains travelling in the proper direction on the running lines, and must not be used for any other purpose, except as provided in Rule 197. Trains moving in the wrong direction on any running line or shunting from one running line to another, or shunting into, or out of, sidings connected with running lines, must, unless fixed signals are provided for such movements, be signalled verbally, or by hand signal, as occasion may require.

HAND SIGNALS.

34. (a)   [Deleted]

(b) A red hand signal indicates Danger and, except as shown below, must be used only when it is necessary to stop a train. In the absence of a red light, any light waved violently denotes Danger.

Exception.

To indicate to Driver that the vacuum requires to be created. (*General Regulations for working the Vacuum Brake.*)

Red light moved vertically up and down above shoulder level.

(c) A yellow hand signal indicates Caution and is used for the following purposes:—

1. To indicate to Driver and Guard during fog or falling snow that a distant signal in which a yellow light is used is at Caution.–Rule 59, 91 and 194.	Yellow hand signal held steadily by Fogsignalman.
2.To indicate to Driver that a distant signal in which a yellow light is used is defective and cannot be placed at Caution.–Rule 81.	Yellow hand signal held steadily by Handsignalman at distant signal.

3. To indicate to Driver that single line working is in operation. –Rule 200.	Yellow hand signal held steadily by Handsignalman at a distant signal, in which a yellow light is used, applicable to the line upon which single line working is in operation.
4. To authorise Driver to pass a multiple-aspect signal which is disconnected or out of order.–Rule 78.	Yellow hand signal held steadily by Handsignalman at the signal.
5. To indicate to Driver and Guard during fog or falling snow that a multiple-aspect signal is at Caution.–Rule 91.	Yellow hand signal held steadily by Fogsignalman.
(d) The purposes for which a white hand signal is used are as follow:–	

(d) The purposes of which a white hand signal is used are as follows:–

1. Move away from hand signal, in shunting.–Rule 52.	White light waved slowly up and down.
2. Move towards hand signal, in shunting.–Rule 52.	White light waved slowly from side to side across body.
3. To indicate to Guard of passenger train that all is right for the train to proceed.–Rule 141.	White light held steadily above the head by person in charge.
4. To acknowledge Guard's green hand signal.–Rule 142, clause (d).	White light held steadily by Fireman
5. To indicate to Signalman that the points require to be turned.–Rule 69.	White light moved quickly above the head by a twisting movement of the wrist, by Guard or Shunter.

NOTE.–The above paragraph 5 does not apply on the Great Western Railway.

6. To indicate to Guard that Driver of train is carrying train staff. (Regulations for working on single lines by train staff and ticket.)	White hand signal held steadily by the Signalman.

(e) **The purposes for which a green hand signal is used are as follow:–**

1. Move slowly away from hand signal, in shunting.–Rule 52.	Green light waved slowly up and down.
2. Move slowly towards hand signal, in shunting.–Rule 52.	Green light waved slowly from side to side across body.
3. Guard's signal to Driver to start, and to indicate that Guard or Shunter has rejoined train. –Rules 55, 141 and 142.	Green light held steadily above the head, or green flag (where used) waved above the head.
4. To indicate by night to Fireman of goods train after starting that his train is complete.–Rule 142.	Green light waved slowly from side to side by Guard from his van.
5. To indicate to Driver that train is divided.–Rule 182.	Green hand signal waved slowly from side to side by Signalman.
6. To give an All Right signal to Driver where there is no starting signal.–Rules 37 and 38.	Green hand signal held steadily by Signalman.
7. To authorise Driver to move after having been stopped at signal box.–Rule 54.	Green hand signal held steadily by Signalman.
8. To authorise Driver to pass signal controlling entrance to the section ahead at Danger, for shunting purposes.–Rule 38.	Green hand signal held steadily by Signalman.
9. To indicate to Driver and Guard during fog or falling snow that the signal is at Clear.–Rules 91 and 127 (xxii.)	Green hand signal held steadily by Fogsignalman.
10. To reduce speed for permanent-way operations.–Rules 60, 127 (xxi.), 217 and 218.	Green hand signal waved slowly from side to side by Hand-signalman.

11.To give an All Right signal to Driver when fixed signal (other than a multiple-aspect signal) is disconnected or out of order.–Rules 78 and 81.	Green hand signal held steadily by Handsignalman at the signal.
12.To authorise Driver to draw forward to signal box when fixed signal is out of order, before Handsignalman has arrived.–Rule 81.	Green hand signal held steadily by Signalman at the box.
13.To indicate to Driver that section is clear, but station or junction is blocked.–Rule 41.	Green hand signal held steadily by Signalman as train is approaching the box or after giving verbal warning.
14.To indicate to Driver of goods train, timed to stop at a station, that there is nothing to pick up, and that if there is nothing to put off the train it need not stop.–Rule 144.	Green hand signal waved slowly up and down.
15.To indicate that catch points, spring points, or unworked trailing points are in right position for train to pass in facing direction.–Rule 196.	Green hand signal held steadily by Handsignalman at points.
16.To caution Driver entering terminal station, or station worked under special instructions, if line is not clear.–Rule 96.	Green hand signal held steadily by Signalman after bringing train to a stand.
17.To caution Driver of following train.–(Regulations for working on goods lines where the Absolute Block System is not in operation or where no special Regulations are in force.)	Green hand signal held steadily by Signalman after bringing train to a stand.

Great Western Company's addition:–

18. To indicate to Signalman after sunset that points require to be turned.

Green hand signal held steadily in the hand by Guard or Shunter at knee level near the points.

London Midland and Scottish Company's additions:–

19. To authorise Driver to pass fixed signal at Danger when attaching, detaching or removing vehicles.–(Rule 116 (b).)

Green hand signal held steadily by the Signalman.

20. To indicate to Guard that Driver of train is carrying ticket.–(Regulations for working on single lines by train staff and ticket.)

21. In the absence of flags–
(a) Both arms raised above the head denotes Danger or stop, thus:–
(NOTE.–*When riding on or in a vehicle either arm moved up and down denotes stop.*)

(b) Either arm held in a horizontal position and the hand moved up and down denotes Caution or slow down, thus:–

(c) Either arm held above the head denotes
All Right, thus:–

(d) Either arm moved in a circular manner away
    from the body denotes move away from
    hand signal, thus:–

(e) Either arm moved across and towards the body at
    shoulder level denotes move towards hand
    signal, thus:–

(f) Arm moved vertically up and down above shoulder level denotes create vacuum, thus:–

20. In shunting operations by night, or when necessary during fog or falling snow, a white light waved slowly up and down means move away from the person giving the signal; a white light waved slowly from side to side across the body means move towards the person giving the signal.

A green light used instead of a white light, indicates that these shunting movements are to be made slowly.

21.(a) Hand lamps and flags, when used as signals, except where they are employed for the purpose of indicating the point of an obstruction, must be held; they must not be placed upon, or fixed in, the ground or elsewhere.

(b)When a Signalman gives a hand signal, it must in all cases be exhibited outside the signal box.

22. After a train has been brought to a stand by a hand Danger signal from a signal box, the Driver must not move, although the hand Danger signal may have been withdrawn, until a green hand signal has been exhibited by the Signalman. This All Right hand signal will not authorise the Driver to pass a fixed signal at Danger unless he has been verbally instructed by the Signalman to do so.

DETENTION OF TRAINS ON RUNNING LINE

24. (a) When a train has been brought to a stand owing to a stop signal being at Danger, the Driver must sound the engine whistle, and, if still detained, the Guard, Shunter or Fireman must (except as shown in the following paragraph, or where printed instructions are given to the contrary go to the signal box and remind the Signalman of the position of the train, and, except as provided in clause (f), remain in the box until permission is obtained for the train to proceed. In clear weather a train must not stand more than three minutes at a stop signal before the man goes to the signal box. During fog or falling snow, unless the stop signal is lowered immediately after the engine whistle has been sounded, the man must at *once proceed* to the signal box.

Where track circuits or electrical depression bars are provided, as indicated on or near the signal posts, or in respect to which printed instructions are issued, and the train is standing on such track circuits or bars, it will not be necessary for the Guard, Shunter or Fireman to go to the Signal box to remind the Signalman of the position of the train, but the engine whistle must be sounded. Where other appliances are provided for the purpose of communicating with the Signalman, the Guard, Shunter or Fireman must immediately make use of such applicances, but if an acknowledgement is not received the provisions of the preceeding paragraph must be carried out.

In the case of single lines, if the Driver is in possession of the trian staff or electric token, it will be necessary for the man to go to the signal box to remind the Signalman of the position of the train in connection with trains detained at home signals, but the engine whistle must be sounded.

(b) When a train or vehicle has passed a stop signal for the purpose of being crossed to another line, or to be let into a siding, or has been shunted on to the opposite running line, or placed on either a main or branch line at a junction, or when a train or vehicle has been shunted from a siding on to a running line for the purpose of being crossed to another line, the Guard, Shunter or Fireman must (except where printed instructions are given to the contrary), when the train or vehicle come to a stand, and is detained, *proceed immediately* to the signal box and remind the Signalman of the position of the train or vehicle, and, except as provided in clause (*f*), remain in the box until the Signalman can give permission for it to proceed to to be shunted clear of the running lines.

(c) The duty of going to the signal box must (except in the case of rail motors, motor trains and electric trains) be performed by the Guard, Shunter or Fireman who is the nearest to the signal box.

TROLLEY WORKING

23. (a) A trolley must only be placed on the line when the Permanent-Way length Ganger, relaying Ganger, Sub Ganger, or other Permanent-Way man in charge is present, and he will be responsible for its proper use and protection. It must not be attached to a train, and when not in use, must be placed well clear of the line, and the wheels secured with chain and padlock, or other authorised means.

(b) Each trolley when on the line must carry a Danger signal which can be clearly seen by Drivers of approaching trains.

(c) A trolley must be used only during daylight and when the weather is is sufficiently clear for the Danger signal on it to be seen at a distance of ½ mile, unless its at other times is unavoidable.

(d) Before a trolley is placed on the line, the Ganger or main charge must, except as provided in clause (l), and as otherwise provided in clause (n) arrange for must, except as provided in clauses (e) and (f), station himself ¾, mile or such further distance as may be necessary, in the rear of the point where the trolley is to be placed on the line, to ensure the Driver of an approaching train having a good and distant view of his hand signal, and he must place on the rail 3 detonators, 10 yards apart, and exhibit a hand Danger signal.

The trolley must not be placed on the line until the Handsignalman is in position.

(e) Should the Handsignalman when going out to protect a trolley arrive at a signal box before he has reached a distance of ¾ mile, he must inform the Signalman what is about to be done and request him to keep at Danger his signals for the line about to be obstructed. The Handsignalman must place on the rail 3 detonators, 10 yards apart, exhibit a hand Danger signal, and remain at the signal box as a reminder to the Signalman of the presence of the trolley until the trolley has been removed or has gone forward ¾ mile from him.

(f) When a trolley is placed on the line between the home signal and signal box or when a trolley which is protected in rear by a Handsignalman enters and comes to a stand upon the line inside the home signal and during the time it remains there, a Handsignalman must be stationed at the box as a reminder to the Signalman of the presence of the trolley, but it will not be necessary to place detonators on the rail.

THE AIMS OF STEAM LOCOMOTIVE RUNNING.

(Taken from 'The Steam Locomotive in Traffic', 1945)

The aim of all railway locomotive operation, irrespective of the form of prime mover employed, is to obtain within any specified period of time the maximum amount of revenue producing work from each locomotive on stock. No one statistical unit has yet been defined which is sufficiently comprehensive to express this condition, the corollary to which is that the stock of power necessary to cover the working of given traffic falls as engine availability increases. The number of hours in steam per engine per annum, a unit which was greatly in favour with the old school of railwaymen, is actually of little value, as it disregards time occupied standing, running light mileage and in other non-revenue earning capacities.

Considering the steam locomotive in particular, the whole of its life from building to scrapping must fall, on analysis, within one or other of the following categories or states:—

(1) In use.

(2) Awaiting depot repairs.

(3) Under depot repairs.

(4) Under depot repairs, awaiting material.

(5) Stopped for boilerwashing.

(6) Awaiting works repairs.

(7) En route to or from works.

(8) Under works repairs.

(9) Available but not in use.

(10) Standing in stock.

(11) On loan to another railway or to a private firm.

The art of locomotive running is to secure an ever increasing proportion of the engine stock in use, together with a corresponding minimum of that stock in states (2)–(10) inclusive. The matter, however, by no means ends here. For example, it is not sufficient that an engine shall merely be in use for a large number of hours each year: its employment must be such that the engine is working as long as possible under the optimum conditions of load and speed for which it has been designed. Further, all work must be so performed by the engine that the total running costs per mile are as low as possible; the total includes such items as supervision, enginemen's wages, fuel, water and lubricants, petty stores and replacements, and maintenance. Constant alertness is necessary in every direction where waste or inefficiency in any other form may arise.

It needs superficial consideration only to reach the conclusion that the attainment of high operating efficiency by no means rests alone with the department responsible for the actual running of the locomotive. Such results can only be obtained by effective co-operation between the several departments concerned and by subordinating their individual interests to those of the railway as a whole. In the first place the design of the engine, quality of the materials used and standards of workmanship exercised during its construction must be such that the engine will run a satisfactorily high mileage between general repairs, be economical as regards its performance and maintenance, and not be liable to failure or to the booking of extensive or recurring running repairs. Again, the furtherance of these same objects demands thorough training of enginemen and efficient supervision of their work, regular and conscientious servicing of the engine by the shed staff, a high standard of workmanship for running repairs and intelligent anticipation, in the shape of examinations, carefully and regularly made at predetermined periods, to prevent the development of defects. Permanent way and signalling installations must be maintained at the required standards and, lastly, the operating department is responsible for the minimisation of delays in traffic, other than those attributable to the locomotive department, and to some extent for the retention of the individual engine on that work which is most appropriate to its characteristics.

As each of the various states in which the steam locomotive may exist will be given detailed consideration subsequently in this work, cursory mention of them will be sufficient at this stage. The minimisation of the percentage of engine stock awaiting or under depot repairs, and stopped for boiler-washing is chiefly a matter of organisation, lay-out and equipment. In the case of engines awaiting material, assuming that the possibility of shed stores being understocked does not arise, co-operation between the running shed and the main works is essential; the works must be promptly and accurately advised of what is required, in advance where possible, and equally quickly fulfil the needs of the case. There is always the possibility that the works, preoccupied with the completion of building programmes and the output of

Fig. 1 **TYPICAL STAFFING ARRANGEMENT OF A LOCOMOTIVE DEPOT**

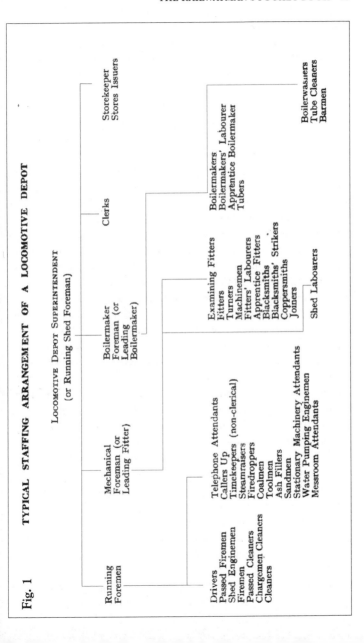

LOCOMOTIVE DEPOT SUPERINTENDENT
(or Running Shed Foreman)

Running Foremen

Mechanical Foreman (or Leading Fitter)

Boilermaker Foreman (or Leading Boilermaker)

Clerks

Storekeeper
Stores Issuers

Drivers
Passed Firemen
Shed Enginemen
Firemen
Passed Cleaners
Chargemen Cleaners
Cleaners

Telephone Attendants
Callers Up
Timekeepers (non-clerical)
Steamraisers
Firedroppers
Coalmen
Toolmen
Ash Fillers
Sandmen
Stationary Machinery Attendants
Water Pumping Enginemen
Messroom Attendants

Examining Fitters
Fitters
Turners
Machinemen
Fitters' Labourers
Apprentice Fitters
Blacksmiths
Blacksmiths' Strikers
Coppersmiths
Joiners

Shed Labourers

Boilermakers
Boilermakers' Labourer
Apprentice Boilermaker
Tubers

Boilerwashers
Tube Cleaners
Barmen

heavy repairs, may at times fail to realise the monetary loss to the railway represented by interest on the heavy capital cost in the aggregate of a number of engines standing idle and awaiting material. In this case a vigorous policy of following up requisitions must be initiated by the running department; temporary improvements may be effected in individual instances by the expedient of exchanging the part concerned with one from another engine which is either under more lengthy repairs or awaiting shops.

The case of engines awaiting works repairs, similarly, is one for co-ordination by running headquarters and the works to ensure a steady flow of engines to shops for general repairs on the one hand and minimisation of time out of traffic for this reason on the other. In any event engines recommended for shops at a specified time should not then be withdrawn from traffic but, provided their individual condition permits them to do so without undue risk of failure, should remain in use, although possibly on considerate work, until they are actually called into shops by the works authorities. With the same stipulations, again applying the principle of extracting the maximum of work from all engines, those which are en route to or from works should, where possible, work trains whilst so engaged.

Improvements in shops lay-out and the installation of modern machine tools and other equipment have revolutionised the time lost from traffic by engines owing to general repairs. For example, engines which a few years ago required three months for a heavy repair can now be turned out in a fortnight. The chief precaution to be taken is that rapid production shall not affect adversely the standard of workmanship, in which event there will be undesirable repercussions on the percentage of engine stock under and awaiting depot repairs, on the mileages run between general repairs and, possibly, on the values of the running stores stocked per engine allocated.

That a certain proportion of the engine stock should be available but not in use is unavoidable, as a margin must always be provided to cover fluctuations of traffic and, also, potential failures. This margin is naturally greatest at depots where freight workings predominate or traffic of a seasonal nature is operated; the effects of this latter condition may be mitigated by temporary transfers of engine power from less busy districts to those where the increased traffic is arising.

The percentage of engine power standing in stock is a reflection of the relative prosperity of the railway as a whole; alternatively it indicates the existence of certain engines for which suitable work is not available.

Fig. 2   TYPICAL LOCOMOTIVE RUNNING HEADQUARTERS ORGANISATION

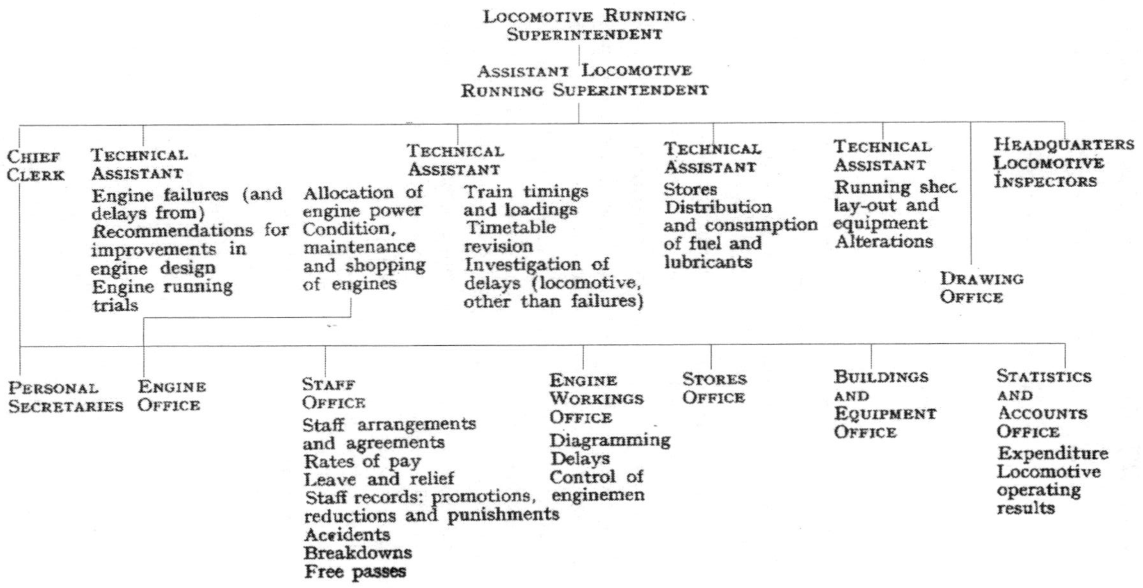

LOCOMOTIVE RUNNING
SUPERINTENDENT

ASSISTANT LOCOMOTIVE
RUNNING SUPERINTENDENT

CHIEF CLERK	TECHNICAL ASSISTANT	TECHNICAL ASSISTANT	TECHNICAL ASSISTANT	TECHNICAL ASSISTANT	TECHNICAL ASSISTANT	HEADQUARTERS LOCOMOTIVE INSPECTORS
	Engine failures (and delays from) Recommendations for improvements in engine design Engine running trials	Allocation of engine power Condition, maintenance and shopping of engines	Train timings and loadings Timetable revision Investigation of delays (locomotive, other than failures)	Stores Distribution and consumption of fuel and lubricants	Running shed lay-out and equipment Alterations	

DRAWING OFFICE

PERSONAL SECRETARIES	ENGINE OFFICE	STAFF OFFICE	ENGINE WORKINGS OFFICE	STORES OFFICE	BUILDINGS AND EQUIPMENT OFFICE	STATISTICS AND ACCOUNTS OFFICE
		Staff arrangements and agreements Rates of pay Leave and relief Staff records: promotions, reductions and punishments Accidents Breakdowns Free passes	Diagramming Delays Control of enginemen			Expenditure Locomotive operating results

DEPARTMENTAL ORGANISATION. FUNCTIONS AND POLICY OF HEADQUARTERS

(a) ORGANISATION.

The primary unit of administration is the locomotive depot or running shed, and a typical example of the staff organisation for such a unit is given in Fig. 1. Actual practice differs slightly on various railways and, further, local conditions sometimes dictate departures from the standard adopted by any given railway. It will be noted in the example given that three shed grades, namely, shed labourers, boilerwashers and tube cleaners, are shewn as under the control of workshops grade supervisors, the nature of their duties making this a convenient arrangement in these instances.

On those railways where the route mileage worked and the number of engines on stock are both small, the arrangement whereby the depot is directly responsible to the headquarters of the department is both convenient and economical. This principle, however, is not suitable for application to a large system as it leads to excessive centralisation of departmental control and, unless other departments are similarly administered, to a corresponding reduction in status of local departmental representation. In order to counteract these two undesirable features it becomes necessary to divide the system, for locomotive operating purposes, into divisions or districts, the extent of each being governed mainly by traffic density and consideration of other operating and geographical conditions. Each depot is then responsible to the divisional or district officer concerned, and the latter to headquarters. Critics of this system argue that district headquarters merely act as sorting offices and that their interpolation between departmental headquarters and the individual depot delays the conduct of affairs. Generalisations are always dangerous, and in these instances, the former, if true, merely indicates the presence of inefficiency, in the district under consideration, which must be eradicated; as regards the latter, although the progress of the individual instruction from departmental headquarters is admittedly delayed by passing through divisional headquarters, the ultimate effect of some such intermediary, making any adjustments necessary to suit local conditions and criticising constructively, is to prosecute affairs to their conclusion in what is eventually the most satisfactory manner. For convenience, the locomotive divisional headquarters should be located at centres coinciding with those of other departments; divisional area boundaries should also coincide for all departments.

The locomotive operating organisation may exist with relation to that of the railway as a whole in three forms, namely:—

(1) As a subsidiary or outdoor section of the mechanical engineer's department.

(2) Under a locomotive running superintendent who is subordinate to the head of the traffic or operating department.

(3) As an independent department, the head of which is directly responsible to the management.

Here again the size of the system is one of the determining factors. It is in the general interest of the railway to minimise the number of departments, but this minimum unavoidably increases with the size of the undertaking. For example, the civil engineer can be responsible for the signalling, telegraph and telephone apparatus on a small railway, in addition to way and works, and the traffic superintendent for the goods and commercial, or traffic getting functions in addition to that of train operation; such measures accomplish economy of supervision, and are therefore justifiable under these conditions, but are not feasible in the case of a large organisation.

As previously mentioned, co-operation, with the authorities responsible for the design, building and heavy repair of the engines on the one hand, and for all engine movements outside the limits of the locomotive depot yards on the other, is essential to the success of locomotive running. Actually, the attainment of this co-operation in its highest form is relatively more important than the actual departmental organisation adopted, but in the last analysis such co-operation in the considered opinion of many is best secured by independence of the locomotive running function as regards both administration and criticism. Subordination of locomotive running to the mechanical engineer's department tends to weaken the contact with traffic operation; when subordinate to this latter function, the converse holds good. A further objection arising with this second alternative is that the traffic operating executives unless, as is rarely the case, they are professionally trained and qualified locomotive engineers, cannot exercise technical control over locomotive running. Unless directly represented there, the locomotive running section should be permitted to intervene with any system of train control which may be in operation to the extent that their specialised knowledge is utilised to prevent missuse of engine power.

The organisation of the locomotive running headquarters is not greatly affected by interdepartmental relationships, and a rep-resentative example is indicated in Fig 2. Each office has of course its clerical staff, with a senior clerk in charge, and the organisation illustrated is appropriate for the control of a total stock of approximately 2,500 engines; modifications would be necessary to make it suitable either for a larger or smaller systems. The same general principles on a smaller scale, to the organisation of divisional headaquarters. In this case tghere are no technical assistants, the more advanced work of this nature being performed by the divisional superintendent and his assistant and the remainder by the mechanical foremen and supernumerary trainees, The number of offices would also be reduced, depending on the size of the division under consideration; in most cases a general office, and offices for engine workings, staff matters and stores suffice. For small districts, all clerical functions may be combined in one office.

LOCOMOTIVE RUNNING SHED EQUIPMENT
COAL HANDLING

The most elementary method of handling coal is direct from the wagon to the tender by manual labour; as the quantity of coal in the wagon diminishes, the side door may be let down and utilised as a working platform, supported by slings of bar iron in preference to a prop, which is unreliable and therefore dangerous. When an intermediate period of storage is unavoidable, the coal is unloaded from the wagon to the ground and thence as required, to the tender, a grab being substituted for manual labour when available and justified by working conditions.

The next development is to elevate the wagon road above the engine road that the wagon door may be dropped on to the coping of the tender. A weighing machine, on which the wagon stands, may be provided and used after each engine is coaled, thus rendering superflous the need for an estimate, which may be of doubtful accuracy, of the amount issued.

Lastly, there is the elevated wagon road with coal stage, where the coal is first unloaded into skips or tubs, usually of ½ ton capacity, and delivered thence as required to the tenders. Generally speaking, no case can be made out for the installation of a mechanical coaling plant at a shed having an allocation of less than 30 engines, and in such instances one or other of the foregoing methods of manual coaling must be retained. The cost of coaling manually from a stage is approximately 50% greater per ton handled than by the direct method from wagon to tender, but a stage is not always avoidable as, for instance, when the period of maximum availability of the coalmen does not coincide closely with that of the peak demand for the issue of the coal. It is not desirable to quote here any general figures or tonnage of coal handled per man per shift; these quantities are governed by local conditions and fluctuate within wide limits.

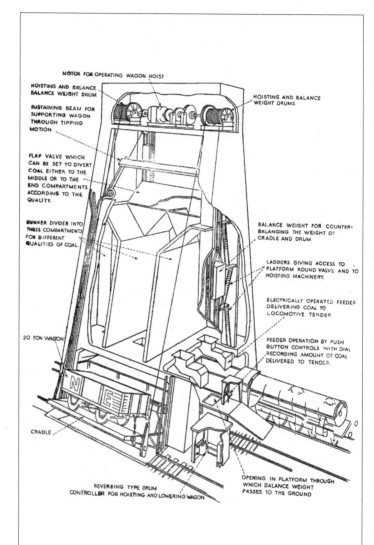

MOTOR FOR OPERATING WAGON HOIST

HOISTING AND BALANCE BALANCE WEIGHT DRUM

SUSTAINING BEAM FOR SUPPORTING WAGON THROUGH TIPPING MOTION

FLAP VALVE WHICH CAN BE SET TO DIVERT COAL EITHER TO THE MIDDLE OR TO THE END COMPARTMENTS ACCORDING TO THE QUALITY.

BUNKER DIVIDED INTO THREE COMPARTMENTS FOR DIFFERENT QUALITIES OF COAL.

HOISTING AND BALANCE WEIGHT DRUMS.

BALANCE WEIGHT FOR COUNTER-BALANCING THE WEIGHT OF CRADLE AND DRUM.

LADDERS GIVING ACCESS TO PLATFORM ROUND VALVE AND TO HOISTING MACHINERY.

ELECTRICALLY OPERATED FEEDER DELIVERING COAL TO LOCOMOTIVE TENDER

FEEDER OPERATION BY PUSH BUTTON CONTROLS WITH DIAL RECORDING AMOUNT OF COAL DELIVERED TO TENDER.

20 TON WAGON

CRADLE

REVERSING TYPE DRUM CONTROLLER FOR HOISTING AND LOWERING WAGON

OPENING IN PLATFORM THROUGH WHICH BALANCE WEIGHT PASSES TO THE GROUND

London and North Eastern (L.N.E.R) Coaling plant at York

THE TURNING OF ENGINES.

In those instances where sufficient space is available, the best method of turning engines is by means of a triangle, the initial and maintenance costs both being markedly less than is the case with a turntable. In its most refined form the triangle is provided with automatic points, thus eliminating the necessity for the fireman to leave the footplate and coincidentally accelerating the turning process. In some instances running sheds are located at approximately right angles to the running roads they serve, with the inlet and outlet roads diverging in opposite directions; with this arrangement an engine coming on shed is turned automatically for a subsequent working in the reverse direction.

When the available area is either insufficient or not of the required triangular form, recourse must be had to a turntable. Modern turntables may be classified in three main categories:

1. *The Centre Balanced Type*, which at present forms the majority in Great Britain, the engine to be turned being so placed on the table that as much as possible of its weight is supported by the centre pivot which, together with its foundation, must therefore be made sufficiently strong to support the total weight of the engine; the attainment of the condition of equilibrium is indicated in practice when the race wheels at both ends of the table are floating freely at an equal height above the race rails. It follows that the necessary diameter of the table must be considerably greater than the wheelbase of the longest engine to be turned, especially when extreme conditions, e.g., an engine with its tender depleted of both water and fuel, are taken into account. The race wheels are given an initial clearance when the turntable is erected, this clearance having to be maintained, and support part of the weight of the engine only in those cases when the engine is not completely balanced on the table; in these circumstances the force necessary to turn the table is considerably increased above that obtaining when the balance is complete. Further, the lifting of the table, necessary to give the race wheels clearance, increases the extent of the shock loads imposed by the engine as it comes on the table, and has a detrimental effect on the costs of maintenance.

As the main girders are virtually cantilevers, they must be of deep section in order to minimise the deflection under load, and a correspondingly deep pit is necessary. The shock loads sustained by the table as an engine enters on to it are taken by blocking pads which, in most designs, are conveniently combined with the locking tongues; the locking movements at each end of the table may be arranged either for independent or combined operation. The extent of the shock loads is governed by the manner in which the engine is placed on the table, by the care with which it is balanced and by its speed of entry; there are unfortunately some enginemen who, when they think they are not being supervised, will run their engine on to the table at an excessive speed, disregarding the rule, which is either to approach with caution or to bring every engine to a dead stand before entering on the table. The purpose of this regulation is not only to minimise the turntable maintenance costs, but also to further the interests of the enginemen themselves, because it emphasises the necessity for them to satisfy themselves that the table is locked before attempting to place an engine on it.

The type of turntable under consideration resolves itself into two subdivisions, (i) the under girder, and (ii) the over girder table. Whilst the first requires a deeper pit than the second, the main girders in this design are not excentrically loaded, as their centres coincide with that of the load on the table top rails. On the other hand the over girder type, although needing only a shallow pit (a not unimportant point where difficulties of pit drainage are encountered) calls for a table of greater width, with the result that the structure is both heavier and more costly.

2. *The Mundt Type*, in which a shallow continuous girder, not of uniform strength, is employed. The girders are reinforced from each end towards the centre pivot, but the reinforcements terminate short of the latter by a predetermined distance. A measure of flexibility is thus provided which, should the weight of an engine be chiefly supported at one end of the table, is sufficient to ensure that the opposite end does not rise; this type of table may therefore be power driven at either end, the total weight of the engine being supported at the centre pivot and by both sets of end wheels. There is no necessity to balance the engine on the table, and only a very shallow pit is necessary.

When compared with the centre balanced type, the following advantages are claimed for the Mundt table:

(a)   Reduced costs of maintenance.

(b)   The overall turning time is reduced, as there is no necessity to balance the engine.

(c)   For the same reason, the necessary table diameter is less for an engine of given wheelbase.

(d)   The pit is of correspondingly less diameter and more shallow.

(e)   The centre pivot and foundation need not be designed to sustain the total weight of the engine.

As the load is normally taken mainly by the end wheels, the turning effort is rather greater than the minimum obtaining with the centre balanced table, but it is claimed that the necessary turning effort compares favourably with that for the articulated type, about to be described, because in the former case the proportion of the total load taken by the end wheels is less.

The time required to turn an engine through 180 degrees by hand with a Mundt ball bearing table is approximately three minutes, and of course less with a power drive.

3. *The Articulated Type* of table, so constructed that each of the main girders consists of two beams attached to one another, and to the pivot, by an articulation at the table centre. These articulations take various forms and are, for instance, of the trunnion type, the hinged plate type or embody laminated spring joints. In any event, the fundamental feature of the design must be that no play shall arise in the joint as the result of driving the table from one end. Should any slackness occur at the joint the race wheels are immediately displaced from their true position, with the result that the necessary extent of the turning effort is increased appreciably.

With this type of table the load is distributed over the centre pivot and the end wheels, which make permanent contact with the race rails and take at least one half the load, the wheels and bearings being of substantial design. In consequence this type of table may be directly driven at either end. The advantages of shallow girders and pits, together with those arising from the elimination of the necessity for balancing the engine, again apply.

The Mundt type is known in this country as the Rapier Mundt turntable and, by the courtesy of the makers, Messrs. Ransomes and Rapier Limited of Ipswich,and can come in various sizes. The general arrangement is of a 65 ft. turntable but they can be slightly smaller at, 60 ft. in diameter. Turning is by electric power with manual auxiliary.

Messrs. Cowans, Sheldon and Co. Ltd., Carlisle, are the licencees for the manufacture in Great Britain of the Vögele type of articulated turntable. This is a general arrangement of a 70 ft. table fitted with a vacuum tractor, which will be described later, and is capable of turning an engine weighing 175 tons through 180 degrees in two minutes. Several tables to this design have been supplied to the LNER.

Irrespective of the type of turntable installed, there are in all cases certain features of design which are either essential or desirable. In the first place the provision of ball bearings for the centre pivot and race wheels has a marked effect on the necessary turning effort. As a general statement, the coefficient of friction for ball bearings ranges from .001 to .0015, and that for a plain bearing from .07 to .08 with intermittent lubrication, or from .03 to .05 when the lubrication is continuous; even with careful design, however, continuous lubrication is difficult, if not impossible to achieve with a plain bearing, and in practice the coefficient of friction is appreciably increased by the fall of atmospheric temperature and the presence of grit or other foreign matter in the bearing. For the race wheels, spindles or axles should be provided to run in ball bearings mounted in the race wheel supporting framework; this is better practice than the alternative arrangement, which is to house the ball bearings in the race wheels themselves and allow them to rotate on a dummy axle. In order to minimise wear the race wheels should be relatively few in number and of comparatively large diameter, a tapered profile being most satisfactory for the treads.

The race wheels and bearings, blocking pads and locking gear must all be readily accessible for inspection, lubrication and repair; this is usually accomplished by cutting away, and boarding over, a rectangular inspection chamber in the pit wall. Ease of access to the centre pivot, including the bolts, is equally essential for the same reasons.

The deck must be as clear and free from obstruction as possible. It should be of sufficient width to provide a passage way on both sides of the engine being turned, and protected. The protection may take the form of handrails or be achieved by completely boarding over the pit; the former arrangement is decidedly to be preferred on the grounds of cost, accessibility and visibility. The table pit must be adequately drained; if the surroundings are unavoidably at a higher level than the coping, a retaining wall or boarding should be provided to prevent ballast or grit being washed down into the pit, where it will block the drains in wet weather. The maximum overhang of an engine being turned under the least favourable conditions must be the criterion when considering the question of obstructions adjacent to a turntable.

All turntables should be thoroughly examined, as regards both the structure and the moving parts, at stipulated regular intervals. The period usually varies from 6 to 12 months, and is governed by the type of table concerned, the frequency with which it is used, and the nature of its use. Careful observation must also be made on the level of all roads serving turntables; further, their radial position must be corrected, if necessary, by slewing. The maintenance of the race rails at their correct level is also essential.

It is frequently found that the older types of turntable become increasingly difficult to turn with age; there are several possible causes for this, such as, for example, the development of a tendency to tilt transversely, and in such instances the fitting of spiders, or outriggers, with supplementary race wheels will usually effect an improvement. When it is desired to increase the diameter of an existing turntable, the best method of doing so is to provide auxiliary main girders and enlarge the pit to suit. In those cases where the extension is relatively great, an additional race, running outside that originally provided, becomes necessary. An arrange-ment of this kind, although more expensive initially, is ultimately more satisfactory than the fitting of lengthening irons which, although they have had wide applications in the past owing to their low first cost, have proved expensive to maintain on account of the excessive deflection and distortion to which they are inherently subject.

Turntables may be operated manually, by electric motor, or by a tractor utilising either the vacuum or compressed air from the engine continuous brake, according to the system in use. It must of course be remembered that an engine standing unbalanced on a table requires a greater force to turn it than one which is balanced, irrespective of the type of table or method of turning it; the modifying effect of the penultimate factor is merely one of degree. The present indications are that manual operation will be limited for the future to the smaller and less frequently used tables. Turning time is appreciably reduced with power operation and the need for reinforced labour to turn an unbalanced engine on a manually operated table does not exist; similarly, the cause of claims under the Workman's Compensation Act, for injuries sustained whilst turning engines, is removed.

Electric operation has been much more widely adopted abroad than in Great Britain; a motor of the totally enclosed traction type is usually employed and located under the deck flooring with the dual objects of protection from the effects of possible derailments and elimination of obstacles from the deck. A cabin is provided for the attendant and the controls; the employment of attendants is relatively expensive and can only be justified when they obviate extensive congestion of engines waiting to turn. The braking of an electrically operated table is not so effective as with a tractor; the horse power of the motors provided is also high by comparison. As a general rule, 10 h.p. motors are fitted to tables up to 80 ft. in diameter on the Continent, although this allowance may be exceeded. Examples from U.S.A. practice are 25 h.p. for a 90 ft. table and two 15 h.p. motors for a 100 ft. table; in these cases the weights of the engines turned are considerably greater than those encountered on the Continent and have corresponding influences on the weights of the turntable structures.

Tractors operated either by the vacuum or air brake on the engines are patented and manufactured by Messrs. Cowans, Sheldon and Co. Ltd., to whom the author is indebted for permission to publish the following description.

The example described by the general arrangement is vacuum operated. The actuating engine is essentially simple, robust and compact, the clearance area required in plan being only 2 ft. 5½in. x 1 ft. 11 in.; the two cylinders, of the oscillating type, have a diameter of 4½ in. with a stroke of 6 in. The engine is directly coupled by a pinion on the crankshaft through gearing to one of the turntable end wheels. The operation of one lever effects both reversal and speed control, the former being obtained by four spring loaded valves of the mushroom type, arranged at the end of the chamber between the cylinders, which open the top and bottom ports either to vacuum or atmospheric pressure. Braking is effected by reversal of the tractor; rough usage leads only to skidding of the driving wheels.

The piston heads are of a light alloy and lubricated by a soft packing ring to which oil is fed as required through suitable nipples. The cylinder covers are hinged, and held in position by a spring loaded crossbar, to facilitate access to these nipples. The piston rod glands are also lubricated with oil. Ball or roller bearings are fitted to the cylinder trunnions and to the crankshaft. Emergency manual gear is incorporated, and consists of a handle attached to the second shaft in the gearing.

When it is required to turn an engine it is placed on the table and its train pipe coupled, by a flexible connection, to a stand pipe located adjacent to the tractor. The vacuum ejector is then placed in the "off" position and turning may be commenced, with the single lever control, when approximately 15 in. of vacuum are available; by keeping the ejector in this position whilst turning, the drop in vacuum on completion is only about 3 in. Actually the tractor will operate with only 5 in. of vacuum. It is possible to turn an engine weighing 150 tons through 180 degrees in approximately 1¼ minutes. The tractors, being self contained and attached to the table by a simple hinge, only requiring the drilling of a few holes, are very easily removed and transferred to another turntable if desired.

The fitting of accumulators, or reservoirs, to ensure a reserve supply of vacuum or compressed air as the case may be, enables the tractor to manoeuvre an unloaded turntable or turn completely an engine which is either dead or not fitted with a continuous brake.

The Locomotiveman's Pocket Book

(Taken from 'London & North Eastern Railway. The Locomotiveman's Pocket Book', 1947)

FOREWORD TO FIREMEN

The object of this book is to assist you to prepare to pass the examination and become efficient Firemen and Drivers. It must be clearly understood that the Inspector may submit questions in an entirely different form from that shown in the book and may supplement the question in order to elucidate a doubtful answer.

This book will help you, but alone will not enable you to pass. You should go to the engine and see that you understand what the book tells you to do, and why you have to do it, i.e., you must be able to apply your knowledge in a practical manner, so that you may be able to find out what is amiss and then deal effectively with it.

Safety must be your first consideration and so you should protect your train in accordance with the Rules and Regulations, and then make the best effort to clear the lines as quickly as possible.

This book deals with the Westinghouse and Vacuum Brakes; the Locomotive, its failures and their remedies. It must be clearly understood that all other information relating to examination will be found in the Rules and Regulations. In your firing experience you will be expected to become conversant with the various working parts of the engine and you may be asked any practical question concerning your duties which a driver ought to know.

Fuel Economy

Instruction to Firemen

This chapter is introduced with a view to assisting Firemen to do their work with knowledge and confidence and so produce the best results with the minimum of physical effort in the most economical manner.

The following paragraphs contain a few practical hints which will be useful to Firemen. The time has come, however, when it is both necessary and wise for Firemen to make themselves conversant with the combustion of coal, so far as the locomotive is concerned. The principal points to be observed are as follows—

When a fireman comes on duty and has examined the water level in the boiler and tested the water gauge cocks, his attention should then be given to the state of the firebox. He should whenver possible, see the tube ends, brick arch and stays are clean, also that there is no leakage from either lead plugs, tubes, stays, etc. He should follow this up by openingthe smokebox door, satisfy himself that there is no leakage at that end of the boiler, that the blast pipe and jet pipe, etc, are in order, that all ashes have been cleaned out and, finally, before gently closing the door, he should wipe its edge and the smokebox beading with a greasy cloth, bearing in mind that it is most essential to make an airtight joint, which materially assists in maintaining steam throughout the journey.

Having satisfied himself that the ashpan has been cleared out and the firebars are in proper order, he can then taken steps to make up his fire.

Great care must be exercised in building up the fire in order to ensure a good supply of steam on the journey. A great deal depends upon the first layer of fire being well burnt through, as to add coal to a fire that is black on the top is to court trouble on the journey, so that every care must be taken in this direction. When the coal already put in the firebox is burnt through more should be added and the fire should be gradually built up until there is

Diagram No. 1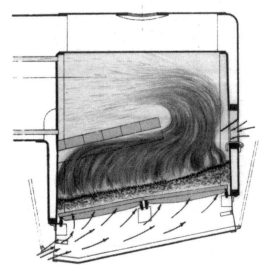

A fire built up as shown above and well burned through would give good results, maintaining steam at high pressure whilst the engine is being heavily worked.

a sufficient body of it, thickest in back corners and under the door, which method is usually satisfactory for the modern engine (see Diagram No. 1).

Coal is of various qualities and compositions, the greater part of it being carbon, the remaining portion composed of gases and ash (see Diagram No. 2). Some coals produce a clinker, which runs to the bars; a good preventative of this is to scatter some limestone or broken fire brick (old brick arch) over the bars before making up the fire. The limestone or fire brick should be broken into pieces not larger than an average sized hen's egg. This not only keeps the metallic substance in the coal from coming in contact with and running to the bars, but it also makes the cleaning of the fire at the end of the journey much easier.

Very large lumps of coal should not be put into the firebox but should be broken to a reasonable size, care being taken not to make too much small or dust. It is easy to imagine what takes place when lumps of coal are deposited against the firebox side, or pushed froward against the tube plate; holes are thus formed allowing cold air to pass through the fire and play upon the plates, setting up local contractions, while the other parts of the firebox are under expansion owing to the heat of the fire, and this inequality will cause the tube ends to leak and thick smoke will be given off.

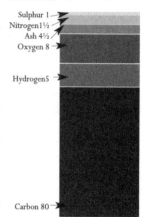

Diagram No. 2
THE AVERAGE COMPOSITION OF STEAM COAL

Sulphur 1
Nitrogen 1½
Ash 4½
Oxygen 8
Hydrogen 5
Carbon 80
TOTAL 100

The excessive use of fireirons on the journey is a bad practice; it is, however, sometimes necessary when commencing the journey to run the pricker lightly through the fire and ease it — also when finishing the run it may be essential to use the bent dart to push the fire from under the door towards the front end in order to burn it down preparatory either to cleaning it or stabling the engine.

Every care should be taken when firing to avoid undue emission of smoke; this should be the Fireman's first consideration. When too much smoke is emitted it means gases are being wasted, resulting in a loss of heat and waste of coal, in addition to causing a public nuisance and complaints from the Health Authorities. The proper method of firing is to fire little and often, especially when using very small coal. To avoid the emission of black smoke from shunting engines, it has been found advantageous to fire alternative sides of the firebox; by this means one half of the fire is kept in a bright state and consumes the smoke emitted from the fire at the other side.

Various quantities of air are required according to the thickness of the fire, and should be regulated by manipulating the damper and firehole door. Air will not flow freely through banks in the fire and combustion at these points will not be satisfactory. Large quantities of air will pass through the thinner parts of the fire and the unburnt gases arising from the banks may not receive a sufficient supply of air to enable them to be burnt, thus allowing gases to pass into the tubes in the form of smoke (see Diagram No. 3). Every Fireman should be aware that the passage of air through the damper and firebars causes rapid combustion of the heated fuel which gives off gases. These gases have to be supplied with air, which enters the firehole door and is directed under the brick arch by the deflector.

The brick arch prevents the gases from escaping unconsumed through the tubes and chimney in the form of black smoke, doing no useful work and choking up the tubes.

There are certain engines which require firing in a way peculiar to themselves. Some engines with horizontal firebars require a level fire;

Diagram No. 3

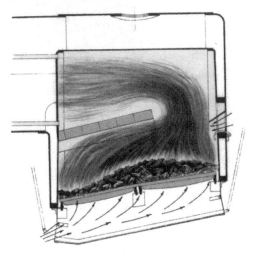

A fire of this kind gives very bad results in maintaining steam, causes a great loss of heat and much smoke.

others require the fire a little thicker at the back end; engines with sloping firebars have a tendency to draw the fire towards the tube plate, and great care must be exercised by quickly turning the shovel and directing the coal into the back corners and under the firehole door. If the fuel is allowed to be drawn off the fire shovel as it enters the firehole door, it will result in an accumulation against the tube plate, as shown in Diagram No. 4.

In all cases it is important that the back of the grate should be covered with fire in order to prevent cold air being drawn through this area and passing direct over the top of the brick arch and thence through the tubes.

Diagram No. 4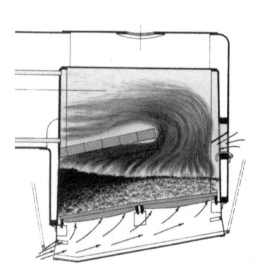

This is an example of bad firing and is absolutely useless, as good steaming results cannot be obtained therefrom.

It is inadvisable to commence firing when leaving a station. The Fireman should first satisfy himself that the train is following in a proper manner. When the engine has started the exhaust will begin to lift and liven the fire, which had settled down after the regulator was closed for making the stop, and then is the time to start firing. A distinct advantage is gained by waiting until the engine is notched up, in order that too much cold air is not admitted to the firebox through the firehole door, as would be the case if firing was taking place when the engine was in full travel.

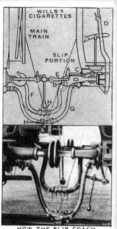
WILLS'S CIGARETTES
MAIN TRAIN
SLIP PORTION

HOW THE SLIP COACH
SYSTEM WORKS

WILLS'S CIGARETTES

MODERN SINGLE LINE
WORKING METHODS

WILLS'S CIGARETTES

MODERN LOCOMOTIVE
COALING PLANT

WILLS'S CIGARETTES

MODERN VACUUM-OPERATED TURNTABLE

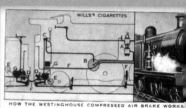
WILLS'S CIGARETTES

HOW THE WESTINGHOUSE COMPRESSED AIR BRAKE WORKS

WILLS'S CIGARETTES

MECHANICAL TRACK LAYER
AT WORK

WILLS'S CIGARETTES

NEXT LIFT

PASSIMETER BOOKING OFFICE

WILLS'S CIGARETTES

LOCOMOTIVE ALONGSIDE
A WATER TANK